THE MALL
An Attempted Escape
from Everyday Life

Jerry Jacobs

Syracuse University

Waveland Press, Inc.
Prospect Heights, Illinois

For information about this book, write or call:

Waveland Press, Inc.
P.O. Box 400
Prospect Heights, Illinois 60070
(312) 634-0081

Printed in the United States of America.

Contents

**To Carin:
Mall Walker Extraordinaire**

Preface

It came to the author's attention a couple of years ago that while there were approximately 23,000 shopping malls in the United States, catering to millions of persons, there was not a single social science book that dealt with this topic.

This work is an attempt to help rectify this oversight. Chapter one gives the reader an introduction into a variety of topics related to mall life that have been treated in various ways in the literature of different disciplines. Chapter two deals with the role of Architects, Developers and Contractors and how they work together to design and build malls. Chapter three orients the reader to the organizational and economic aspects of mall life. Chapter four presents an ethnographic case study of a mid-size enclosed suburban shopping center, and shows how the abstract and formal features discussed in chapters two and three apply to an actual mall setting. Chapter five deals with what many mall customers actually do on the mall, apart from shopping. That is to say, this chapter deals with the social as opposed to the commercial aspects of mall life. These aspects and their implications for the greater society are also dealt with.

In summary, this book presents a documentary and ethnographic study of shopping malls in the United States and their profound influence on transforming our urban and suburban landscapes. The social psychology of mall social life is considered along with its potential effect upon the larger society. The latter treats the malls economic influence, while the former considers the mall as a potential resource for bored urbanites or suburbanites in their attempt to escape from the boredom, trivia or rigors of everyday life.

Chapter 1
Introduction to Shopping Malls

Probably nothing characterizes the change in American cities and suburban areas in recent history so much as the growth and expansion of large indoor shopping malls. These provide shopping, recreational, social, and respite places for persons of all ages and socioeconomic backgrounds.

Some indication of their growth is the fact that while there were 16,400 shopping centers in 1975, there were 22,750 in 1981 (*Wall Street Journal*, April 21, 1982). To get some idea of their relative size, "small" shopping centers are defined as having 25,000 to 400,000 square feet of gross leasable area (G.L.A.), intermediate 400,000 to 600,000 square feet, and large centers 600,000 or more square feet of gross leasable area (*Wall Street Journal,* April 21, 1982).

Such facilities are usuall strategically located near large populations of potential shoppers and adjacent to major roadways. In addition to the ease of access this provides, large areas are set aside for convenient parking. One study by the Urban Land Institute of Washington, D.C., indicates that because of the larger number of smaller cars, and a shift in shopping habits, (more women are employed and shop during the evening) the space devoted to parking lots may be excessive. It is estimated that since 1965 the actual parking space required per 1000 square feet of gross leasable shopping center space is down 27% for small shopping centers, 19% for intermediate, and 9% for large ones (*Wall Street Journal,* April 21, 1982).

Shopping centers now account for about half of all the annual retail sales in the United States within the categories of general merchandise and clothing (Feagin, 1982). This is particularly impressive when we realize that it was not until the 1950's that the first large regional shopping centers were built — usually around a core of major department stores. Nine out of 10 existing malls are less than 20 years old (Feagin, 1982).

Historical Background

A forerunner of the enclosed shopping mall was the development and expansion of arcades in the 19th century. These were built as a way to deal with the increasingly hostile public environments of urban centers. Enclosed

1

shopping centers of this kind were preceded by the agora of Athens, Roman forums and oriental bazaars (Gruen, 1973). A more contemporary example is the pre World War II development of suburban shopping facilities in the 1930's and 40's, such as the Country Club Plaza in Kansas City, Missouri or Westwood Village in Los Angeles. However, these differed from modern regional shopping malls in several ways. For example, they did not feature large department stores, but included office space for a variety of nonmercantile businesses, and because their development preceded the radical expansion of the use of the automobile characteristic of the post World War II period, they had little space allocated for parking (Gruen, 1973).

The post World War II boom period produced an abundance of automobiles, cheap gas, and a population of employed workers able and anxious to purchase them. This in conjunction with the expansion of suburban bedroom communities and an eager buying public, produced the beginnings of the "flight to suburbia" by automobile. Following this mass exodus of people from the central city on their trek to suburbia went the reluctant merchants and department store owners formerly situated in the downtown areas. These located themselves along arterial roads forming the development of many a "Miracle Mile" or "Strip."

Shopping establishments of this kind presented something of a dilemma. The arterial roads, intended to move millions of cars daily from suburbia to urban centers and back again, were being used to relocate shopping centers, which were intended to stop automobiles. With time, this caused monumental traffic jams, which led merchants to develop auxiliary parking in the rear of the store. Customers now started for the first time to routinely enter the store from the rear of the building. This development, the extension of parking facilities and entrances at the rear of the store (as well as the front) were all innovations that were eventually incorporated into contemporary shopping malls (Gruen, 1973). Finally, the success and proliferation of regional shopping centers all contributed not only to the eventual demise of "miracle Mile" shopping, but the deterioration of shopping in urban centers.

To get some idea of the relative unanticipated economic success of indoor shopping malls among early developers (Circa, 1950) we have presented below a section of a case study by architect Victor Gruen (1973).

> "When Webber (the architect's client with J.L. Hudson Co.) teasingly asked Larry Smith (the economist that the client had hired to estimate the malls potential business volume) how it was possible that he could underestimate the gross income of a center in which the first year's business was double ($100 million) the one which he (Smith) had forecast for the fifth year ($50 million) Smith was able to give him a very convincing explanation. "Sir," he said, "I am only an economist; I can

only judge on the basis of past experience; I was not aware of the potentials of the new type development you were creating. However, if you ask me the next time, I will be able to give you the correct answer.''

Whether or not economists have become more successful in predicting the relative success or failure of shopping malls based upon past experience is a topic that will receive further consideration in different contexts throughout the book.

Malls: A Diversity of Professional Interests

In light of the fantastic growth and expansion of shopping centers and their impact upon the urban and suburban scene (rural regional shopping malls are also expanding), there has been a great deal of interest generated in malls. Some indication of the wide-ranging diversity of this interest can be had from a perusal of a sampling of published literature on malls. For example, environmentalists are concerned with the effects of shopping malls on Barrier Beaches (Arehart, 1979) or Vermont's character (Green, 1978). On the other side of the environmental coin, malls may benefit from reduced heating bills in Nottingham, England, as a result of a district heating scheme designed to burn garbage (Lawson and Mason, 1974).

While the expansion of malls is usually held to generate business and increase local revenues (*Business Week,* February 23, 1976), it frequently contributes to the deterioration of downtown areas and small business (Ircha, 1981). If little has been done in the U.S. to protect small businesses from the expanding influences of shopping malls, the Canadian government is moving in the direction of taking protective action (Lang, 1981).

It is not only small businesses external and/or adjacent to shopping malls that are concerned with competition. Even large national department stores within the mall complex (which are least vulnerable) are concerned with competition from discount department stores (*Business Week,* December 8, 1975). This has led to the increasingly popular idea of building separate discount shopping malls, to help eliminate competition within conventional mall settings.

The growth and influence of shopping malls is not solely a national phenomenon. Articles dealing with the international expansion of shopping malls in London (*The Director,* March 1977), the Virgin Islands (Teschler, 1980), and Canada (Baird and Sampson, 1981), as well as other locals, are increasingly found in the literature.

Psychologists and psychiatrists have also become interested in the public's behavior in mall settings. There are, for example, studies of "the effects of sex and smoking on reactions to spatial invasion at a shopping mall" (Bleda and Bleda, 1978); or "Density and Personal Space in a Field Setting" (a mall), (Harris et al., 1978); or the use of stairs versus escalators in malls, "Evaluation and modification of exercise patterns in the natural environment" (Brownell et al., 1980).

There is extensive literature on violence in television programming and its later effects upon children's aggressive behavior. More recently this concern has been supplemented by a concern for whether or not the proliferation of electronic games found in shopping mall arcades is also contributing adversely to childhood socialization. First there is the arcade setting and the "undesirable element" it sometimes attracts and its influence upon the child. Special attention has been given to those trafficking in drugs. Next is the question of the violent nature of electronics games themselves, and how it may affect the child's future behavior (Syracuse Herald-American, Sunday, May 5, 1982). More recently, orthopedists have discovered a new syndrome associated with the prolonged playing of electronic games that affects the mobility of the thumb and wrist in much the same way that "tennis elbow" may result from playing tennis. Other medical studies indicate players (while playing) suffer from elevated blood pressure and heart rates.

Shopping malls have become popular not only with shoppers and retailers but with investors (*Business Week,* October 13, 1980). Buying into a limited partnership in shopping malls has proven for many investors a very lucrative arrangement. Annual yields of 17 to 25 percent are not unusual. The average annual yield during the 1970's was more than 30%. "In 1981, the biggest year for limited partnership investments in real estate, the total investment by large syndicators reached more than one billion dollars, of which 20% was in shopping centers..." (Barmash, 1982).

The above examples are offered for illustrative purposes only, and to give the reader some idea of the current diversity of interest in trade, discipline, and professional books and journals. A more complete set of references is provided at the back of the book.

Shopping Malls: Within and Without

An indoor shopping mall may be defined in a number of ways. One way, sufficient for the purpose of this introductory section, is to view it as a conglomerate of retail stores linked together by enclosed walkways or corridors. Each end of the mall has its "endcaps," "majors," or "anchors" — major national department stores designed both to draw people from the outside world into the mall world, and at the same time contain them between the two end points and thus provide adequate foot traffic for the smaller stores. In the event the "strip" is too long and the "anchors" too far apart, one may be placed at the end, and the other in the middle in order to maximize the drawing potential for the smaller stores.

Malls come in many architectural designs and configurations. Some are simply long rectangles running parallel to large parking lots, while others are shaped like an "L," an "H," or "T". Many are one-story, but some have two or more floors. Depending upon where they are built and the changing complexion of the area, malls are designed to cater to upper, middle, or working class clientele. This is reflected in their architecture, the composition of retail stores, and the extent of security and mall maintenance. Some of the basic configurations of mall designs are given in Chapter 2 (Carpenter, 1978).

While most shopping centers have grown in size horizontally, some more recent ones (especially in urban settings with high land values) have grown vertically. One such mall in West Los Angeles, and bordering on Beverly Hills, is built on a scant 8.5 acres, is eight stories high, and was constructed at a cost of one hundred million dollars. Early reviews are mixed. Like most mall developments the good news is the economic benefits to those in the immediate areas (if one overlooks the adverse effect on small business). The bad news is that this particular development is considered an "eye sore," and promises to promote parking and traffic control problems. There is also the threat to adjacent established upper class shopping facilities on the Miracle Mile (Getlin, February 4, 1982). Primarily intended to cater to an upper class clientele (Bullocks, and The Broadway are the major department stores) this mall when fully completed, will have 14 restaurants, 12 fast food concessions, 16 movie theaters, and 200 other retail shops (Getlin, February 4, 1982). This and the recent development of the Santa Monica Mall, are examples of the expanding number of large urban based shopping malls being built in an effort to attract shoppers back to urban centers and counteract the mass exodus that resulted from the expansion of suburban mall development.

As previously noted, malls cater to different clientele. For example, in upper class malls such as the Chestnut Hill Mall of suburban Boston, the major department stores are Filene's and Bloomingdale's. Between these anchor points one sees only fashionable men's and women's stores like Sachs, I. Magnin, and Brooks Brothers. The architecture is modern, two-story, and avantgarde. By comparison a middle class mall such as Shoptime in "Old Town" (part of this study to be described in greater detail later) is capped by J.C. Penney's and Dey Brothers (Allied Department Stores). Here the architecture is more pedestrian, using long, low corridors of a modified L-shaped design. Finally, the Fingerlake Mall outside of Auburn, New York, may be classified as primarily a working class mall. It has a basic "T" design with Penney's at one end, K-Mart at the other, and Sears at the third end of the "T."

While upper class malls may be standouts in terms of their architectural design and the clientele they cater to, middle and working class malls are frequently defined primarily by the caliber of national department stores that anchor them. This is true because most mall tenants are smaller retail chain stores. This contributes to a certain standardization, sameness, or gray-on-gray quality that large indoor shopping malls seem to exhibit. There is a distinct sense of dèja vue, and one feels that one has seen it all or been there before, no matter where the mall is located or its architectural design.

A friend of mine recently put it this way: "When I'm in a shopping mall, I sometimes forget what season it is or what city I'm in." It is easy to see how this is possible. For example, in women's wear, many East Coast malls have a Lerners, Tops 'n Bottoms, Barbara Moss, Ups 'n Downs, or Foxmoor Casuals. Most have a Kinney, Thom McAn, Florsheim, Altiers, and Connie's shoe store. National jewelry chains such as Kay Jewelers are standard fair. Fast food chains, such as Arbies, McDonald's, Burger King, and Baskin Robbins are everywhere. And, men's wear stores such as Wells & Coverly, Charney's, or Tops n' Bottoms add to the sense of sameness.

It is not just the same names of national chains, but the same signs telling you of it, the same interiors and the similar merchandise displayed in similar ways that contributes to the feeling that, if you've seen one Burger King or one Thom McAn, you've seen them all. All of this is accentuated by the ubiquitous subliminal effects of Muzak or "dentist music."

The above, as well as other features to be discussed in later chapters leave one with the distinct impression that if malls are convenient and pleasant (easy to reach, warm in winter, and cool in summer), they are boring. The overall affect registered by regular adult mall customers is consistent with this overall effect, and may be characterized as the "blase" look (Simmel, 1950). Small children and teenagers prove the exception. How and why this is so will be dealt with later.

Low Maintenance Interiors and Exteriors

Malls are designed and constructed with one major goal in mind—to make money. One way architects and contractors strive to achieve this goal for the builder is to minimize overhead in the form of maintenance costs. Building materials widely used in shopping mall construction mirror this interest. Brick, tile, plastic, glass, stainless steel, composition board hung from suspended ceilings, and unpainted concrete are some examples.

Fast food establishments have the construction of low maintenance facilities down to a science. Everything is tile, plastic or stainless steel, including the tables and chairs or benches. They are easily washed and mopped, and are virtually indestructible. However, they are also standard in their design and execution, and make for a spartan, hard, sometimes garrish form of standardized interior.

The exterior of malls also has that routine low maintenance look in the name of standardizing design and keeping building and maintenance costs down. One rarely sees in the outside segments of the mall, grass, flowers or landscaping of any sort. Green belts are conspicuously absent. From the outside looking toward the center of attraction, one sees only acres of macadam and concrete (the parking lot and entry streets), punctuated by concrete or aluminum light poles. I do not wish to overstate the matter. It is not that shopping malls do not have the look of medieval cathedrals or ivy league campuses. They do not even have the more interesting interior or exterior look of the better designed old-fashioned department stores they seek to replace. Nor is the area surrounding the shopping mall as interesting as "downtown" used to be.

All of this adds to the ho-hum look of mall environments. Inasmuch as millions of people spend a fair portion of their life there, it also contributes to the customers' ho-hum existence. Indeed, this feature is reciprocal and cumulative. It is the ho-hum aspect of suburban everyday life that draw people to malls, and then contributes to escalating the level of ho-humness that one experiences within the mall. This in turn leads one in increased desperation to revisit the mall. These feelings of alienation and the contribution of low maintenance building to those feelings has been the topic of one of the author's former works (Jacobs, 1974). Here the standardization found in single family retirement homes (the "Levittown" look) and "low maintenance yards," i.e., yards of crushed rock and plastic bushes, produces an overall gray-on-gray effect reminiscent of shopping malls.

Finding Your Way: The Ins and Outs of Shopping Malls

We indicated earlier how getting to and from the shopping center and finding easily available parking while there contributes to the overall convenience of patrons and makes shopping, if not exciting, then at least trouble-free. While in part true, this is something of an oversimplification. The novice to the large shopping mall is confronted by much the same problem that travelers have in strange countries or in large unfamiliar cities when trying to find their way around in a different subway system, train station, or airline terminal.

The novice mall-goer must also overcome these problems and does so by invoking ad hoc search procedures. As a potential mall shopper you must:

1. Find your way to the mall from where you are.
2. Find your way into the parking lot, and end up somewhere near where you intend to shop.
3. Once in the mall, find your way to the particular store or stores where you wish to shop.
4. In order to accomplish #3, first become aware of the fact that a

map and directory exist and how to use it.

5. Find your way back to your car in the acres of cars that surround the shopping center.

6. Find your way out of the lot and into the more familiar surroundings of the city streets.

One may protest, "I do this all the time with no trouble at all." However, you must try to remember your first time at the mall to see how these problems apply. The fact is many people do get lost, or lose their cars, their belongings, or their children while shopping at the mall. The occasional announcements over the P.A. system for lost children attest to this. What's more, some of these unfortunates are seasoned shoppers and regular mall customers who routinely encounter the mall and its surroundings as familiar turf. Problems of this kind may in part be responsible for customers returning, time and time again to familiar malls, and offer a kind of time lag problem to the establishment of new ones.

That people also misplace their cars can be shown from police accounts. In a discussion of how crime rates are sometimes artifacts of routine police practices used to generate these rates, Pfuhl (1980) gives as an example police stories of how they are frequently called upon to find a stolen car when someone has in fact only misplaced it in the parking lot of a shopping mall. Having found the car, they sometimes report it stolen and found, as opposed to misplaced by the owner. This makes for inflated rates of "stolen cars," which is good for justifying police business, as well as the role of the police in returning stolen property to its rightful owner.

In any case, looking for someone or something in a 60-acre shopping mall is no easy matter, especially for the novice (*Chain Store Age,* 1973). People often make a conscious effort to note landmarks in order to find their way back to the right exit, the general vicinity of their parked car, and/or note times and places to meet in order to be able to rejoin others later. These and other efforts not to get lost or lose someone or something take a lot of structuring on the part of mall shoppers. They also generate a lot of grief when things go awry.

Getting Into Business: Choosing and Renting Mall Space

In keeping with our preliminary discussion, how does one go about leasing space in a shopping mall? Each mall large enough to warrant it has a mall manager who works for a realty company and is paid to manage the mall. Their job is to contract for people to keep the mall clean and well-maintained (structurally and cosmetically), provide for security, and act as go-between for potential tenants and the leasing agent as well as the mall owners and tenants and the greater community.

The cost of renting mall space depends on how old the mall is, where it is located, where on the mall one wishes to rent, how large an area, and how big a potential draw the would-be renter promises to be for existing or future mall business. Rents in existing malls for small stores range from $6 to $12 per square foot per year, while rents for small stores in new malls typically run between $15 and $20 per square foot (Barnash, 1982). Small store owners (especially those not a part of a national chain), look for things they believe will generate business in choosing a mall, for example, the presence of large (the bigger, the better) national or popular local or regional department stores in the anchor positions, the presence of smaller national chain stores, the extent and kind of population in the adjacent areas, the absence of large discount stores (to give stiff competition and require more sales and lower prices), and location within the mall. Small, independent shopowners must be particularly careful, for they are particularly vulnerable. They are not a part of a national chain, where one store doing well can support another doing poorly, in terms of the chain's net profit. Failure for the small, independent store is absolute and not relative to other possible successes. Indeed, this is well-understood by mall owners who let stores to national chains. Smaller national chain stores are sometimes required to lease store space in undesirable malls — malls that tend to show little or no profit — in order to be allowed to rent space in successful malls. If smaller chains are sometimes discriminated against in this way, large, anchor, national chain stores are frequently given preferential treatment.

Malls are leased in three basic ways: 1. The leasee pays X dollars per square foot plus a percent of gross sales; 2. space is rented strictly by the square foot; or, 3. space is rented, in effect, on credit — that is, the leasing agent agrees to get a higher percentage of all gross sales only. In this case the rent is problematic and represents a gamble for the leasing agent. Currently, because of the popularity of shopping malls, few are leased in this way. Most mall rentals and leases are established according to the first two formulas and such unofficial considerations, as are indicated above, with respect to large national chain stores.

Staying in Business: Playing It by Ear

Choosing a winning mall is a very iffy business. Interviews with independent mall shopkeepers has led me to believe that one's choice and/or future success in business is very problematic. While there are, as indicated above, certain accepted rules of thumb to follow in choosing a mall and a place on the mall, the routine running of a business is done primarily according to common sense recipes and not abstract principles.

For example, one tries some set of products, displays, advertising, and sales; and, if items move and show a profit, one continues in the same vein. If not, one varies the products, the advertising, or the sales items until one begins to show a profit. This approach applies more to independents than to the more standardized format of the national chain stores.

Without going into a detailed description at this point of the merchant's pragmatic approach to business, a brief example (including how they sometimes trade secrets) seems in order. A friend whose father owns a number of jewelry stores in different malls related the following story: a friend of his father's (also a jeweler) was about to run a sale. He, in turn, has a friend who recently ran a successful sale at his jewelry store. The second friend attributes the success of his sale to his radio advertisement, and more particularly to the announcer he got to do the commercial. The first friend hires the same announcer to do his radio commercial. His sale is also a success. Result — my friend's father hired this same out-of-town person for $800 to do a radio commerical for a sale he is planning. The bottom line — why tamper with success?

Using common sense, or "playing it by ear" approaches to rational profit-making, as opposed to elegant economic theories, may not be a bad strategy. After all, one economic theory, "the random walk" theory, holds that with respect to playing the market, future stock prices can't be predicted. In this view...."a Wall Street expert is no more likely to outsmart the market than is a monkey picking stocks by throwing darts" (Blustein, 1982). Another economic-social psychological theory for profit-taking proposed by Professor Shacter based upon "bubba psychology" (a bubba is a Jewish grandmother) also holds that the market does not work on rational principles, but for differernt reasons than those proposed by the "random walk" theory. In either case, according to some experts, the pursuit of profits through the invocation of rational economic models does not seem to hold much promise (Blustein, 1982).

Mall Business and the National Economy

Success in small business is always very problematic, even in malls. This is especially true at the time of this writing, i.e., during a recessionary period. A recent newspaper article notes: "In Federal bankruptcy court in Houston, 3,859 new cases were filed last year, reflecting the recession, up from 995 two years earlier"..."In its sister court in Los Angeles...the clerk noted (an increase) of 86% more (bankruptcies this year) than a year before" (Wall Street Journal, Thursday, May 6, 1982).

The negative effects of recessionary periods are felt not only in the small business sector, but among large national chains as well. For example,

Woolworth's, a national chain with many stores located in mall settings, had its net income plummet 47% in the fourth quarter ending January 31, 1982, and sought as a result to reduce its size by about 30 stores (Wall Street Journal, Thursday, March 11, 1982).

Shrinkage: A Chronic Problem

Shopkeepers, in addition to having to worry about the state of the national economy, attracting customers, staging successful sales, and the selection and display of goods, are also confronted by the chronic problem of "shrinkage" or theft. Shoplifting in malls, or in stores not a part of malls, represents a considerable problem for retailers. The traditional solution was insurance, and passing the cost of the losses through theft on to the customer. However, this is subject to diminishing returns. The increased cost of merchandise ultimately results in fewer sales and lower profits. Apart from increasing insurance coverage retailers have more recently invoked all sorts of anti-shoplifting measures.

Signs are now everywhere telling potential shoplifters that they will be prosecuted. More uniformed and plainclothes security people have been hired. Electronic surveillance systems have been installed that can set off alarms when special tags attached to merchandise have not been properly removed in the course of normal purchase transactions, and one-way mirrors and closed circuit T.V. are used to visually monitor customers. Signs tell would-be buyers and/or shoplifters that only one garment at a time can be tried on, and in some stores salespersons accompany customers into fitting rooms.

The greatest source of shrinkage is generally believed by the public to result from shoplifting customers. However, the facts are otherwise. It is generally agreed in security circles that employees account for more shrinkage than customers. Nor does the caliber of employee (in terms of age or socioeconomic status) seem to reduce shrinkage as one might intuitively imagine. For example, an article in the *Wall Street Journal* a few years ago reported the heavy shrinkage Bloomingdale's department store on Long Island was experiencing around Christmas time. Knowing that employees accounted for more of it than customers, they thought that hiring a better quality of supplemental part-time help to handle the increased volume of customers at Christmas time would help reduce the shrinkage. Instead of hiring high school students (their usual practice), they hire moonlighting teachers and middle class housewives. The results—alas—shrinkage increased dramatically.

All shrinkage is not the result of missing merchandise. In fact bigger losses are frequently sustained by "creative bookkeeping" on the part of in-house employees. For example, a recent newspaper article notes:

> A bookkeeper diverted $750,000 of bill payments to her bank account in three years. Another bookkeeper made off with $80,000 in less than a year by drawing checks to herself and forging the owner's signature on them. A fellow in charge of paying bills paid himself $250,000 of company money. An employee of 28 years, who was a crackerjack at filling and shipping orders, shipped thousands of dollars of merchandise to himself.

The article concludes that according to one authority, if there is a moral to all of this, it is that, "Poorly paid employees may feel justified in ripping off their employer...Pay your employees a fair wage. Otherwise, expect a lot of grief." (Jacobs, May 10, 1982).

How effective are the above efforts at reducing shrinkage? One study by Professor Michael Mills at the University of Southern California indicates "that one person in four is more likely to try to 'beat the system' in heavily-guarded stores" (Syracuse New Times, 1982). It may well be the case that the harder the store tried to reduce shoplifting, the harder the would-be thief tries to increase it. Where this mutual escalation of effort will end is hard to say.

The Mall: Public Space and Public Service

As indicated earlier, malls are constructed to generate profits for the owners of private property. However, in part by design and in part as a "latent function" of this effort, malls may in some ways serve the public interest. For example, malls may contain public or private service facilities such as rest rooms, libraries, post offices, state employment agencies, Army recruitment stations, T.V. stations, banks, and supermarkets. These and other services are considered by many mall users to be public conveniences, i.e., services they routinely require to conduct their normal round of business. In this regard they are glad to find them located in mall settings where they feel that they are obliged to go almost daily, for one reason or another.

In addition to these public conveniences, there are displays that are open to the public and are provided free of charge. For example, there are arts and crafts shows, boat shows, car shows, industrial arts shows (displaying the wood and metal shop project of middle and high school students), magic shows, lion-taming acts, and other performances.

Malls are also used by older people for exercise. Programs sponsored by local hospitals, the American Heart Association or the local "Y" provide for the use of malls by "mallwalkers" in the early a.m. hours before the stores open and the mall is officially in business.

Apart from offering an exercise area for older persons, the mall offers this age group something just as important, a safe haven — a place to spend time, shop, or socialize with others. Many older people consider the downtown shopping area to be an unsafe stretch of public domain, especially in early morning or late evening hours. The elderly are, in fact, vulnerable and prime targets for thefts or muggings.

Perhaps the greatest perceived public service that malls provide is offering bored suburbanites and others, "somewhere to go and something to do." Since the average American now spends seven hours a day watching television, if one fills in or "kills" another three to four hours on the mall, and sleeps seven or eight, the few hours of consciousness remaining become manageable and one is able to "cope."

Some indication of the extent and variety of public mall activity can be had by perusing a typical monthly calendar of events at one of the local malls studied by the author (page 14).

Mall Life: Nothing Unusual Is Happening

To add to the physical sense of sameness one experiences upon the mall, there is the question of the kinds of people who go to malls and what they do when they get there. Shopping in a suburban mall is different from shopping in an urban downtown area. This is so not only because of th deja vue sensation generated by the same stores, same signs, or architectural or design similarities, but also because of the nature of interaction on malls and the persons engaged in them. Mall social life is generally characterized by "nothing unusual is happening" (Emerson, 1969).

Unlike the variety of people one might encounter in a downtown area, one does not encounter vagrants, drunks, prostitutes, street people, ex-mental patients, the retarded, or many blacks or ethnics in suburban mall settings. Indeed, stigmatized persons of any description are conspicuous by their absence. While many shoppers may welcome this homogeneity of "normal people" (respectable-looking and properly behaved persons), it is nevertheless a condition that contributes substantially to the drabness of mall life. Indeed, in this regard, the feeling one encounters in shopping malls is not unlike that one experiences in upper middle class retirement settings (Jacobs, 1974).

There is very little "local color" in malls. Reporters rarely pick shopping malls as a setting for a "human interest story." Given that nothing unusual is happening in malls, there is little of interest to report. While one might, as the author has done in another context (Jacobs, 1979), view the completeness of nothing unusual happening as itself something unusual happening (in shopping malls) this has not yet been done.

APRIL, 1982

SUNDAY	MONDAY	TUESDAY	WEDNESDAY	THURSDAY	FRIDAY	SATURDAY
			Visits with the Easter Bunny April 1-10. Photos available	1 Craft Show and Sale	2 Craft Show and Sale	3 Craft Show and Sale
4 Craft Show and Sale	5 New Boat Show	6 New Boat Show Kayak Pool to be given away	7 New Boat Show	8 New Boat Show	9 New Boat Show	10 New Boat Show
11 Easter Sunday Mall Closed	12	13	14 International Lions Shows 2 & 7 p.m.	15 International Lions Shows 2 & 7 p.m.	16 International Lions Shows 2 & 7 p.m.	17 International Lions Shows 2 & 7 p.m.
18 International Lions Shows 1 & 3 p.m.	19	20 Spring Car Review	21 Spring Car Review	22 East Mino Stage Band 7 & 8 p.m. Spring Car Review	23 Spring Car Review	24 Arthur Murray Dance Demonstration 1 & 3 p.m. Spring Car Review
25 Spring Car Review	26 Spring Car Review	27 Spring Car Review	28 Spring Car Review	29 Spring Car Review	30 Spring Car Review	Spring Car Review May 1st & 2nd

Some indication of the general acceptance of the sense of security and respectability that malls offer can be had from the taken-for-granted way in which middle class parents allow their teenage children to go to shopping malls, while requests to go elsewhere are treated problematically.

All of the front stage impression management required to produce this sense of mall gentility says nothing of the backstage collaboration necessary to sustain it (Goffman, 1959). This will receive further consideration in our future discussion of mall security.

Shopping Malls as Street Corner Societies

In 1943 William Foote Whyte, a sociologist, published what was to become a classic in the field, *Street Corner Society* (Whyte, 1943), and dedicated it to "The Corner Boys of Cornerville." Twenty-four years later, an anthropologist named Elliot Liebow published a book called *Tally's Corner* (Liebow, 1967). This too became something of a classic in the field.

While Whyte conducted an ethnographic study of teenage gangs in Boston and Liebow, an ethnographic study of black street corner men in Washington, D.C., these studies had (apart from their methodology) much in common.

Both were concerned with how two different sets of persons, in different cities, in different age groups, and at different times dealt with the question of unemployment/or underemployment, free-time, self-esteem, and boredom, by searching out and establishing routine meaningful forms of everyday social life. In a formal sense, shopping malls may be seen as a modern extension of these efforts for a completely different socioeconomic class's search for a street corner society. This is true for teenagers now as it was in Whyte's time. But now, more than before, it is not only teenagers and blacks who are unemployed or underemployed (Total male teenage unemployment in 1979 was 15.8%—34% for black teenagers; U.S. Department of Labor, 1979) but the growing top of the age pyramid—older retired persons. Add to this white unemployed middle class suburban housewives, and the mall is a new haven for those who are bored, disenfranchised, and loaded down with "dead time." Such persons are looking, if not for action, then at least distraction. We will deal in future chapters with the way in which the mall serves these different age groups, and social classes in their search for meaning and their flight from boredom.

Shopping Malls: Stable Institution or Passing Fad?

We have sketched some of the features of mall life, their phenomenal expansion, and their ubiquitous effect upon American social life. The question presents itself, "Are malls here to stay, or are they a flash-in-the-pan?"

Given their numbers, costs, and economic and social effects upon the physical and social landscape, there is reason to suppose that malls will be here for some time to come. After all, vested interests on this scale have a momentum all their own. But, like most things, malls too will pass; and the long-range question is not "if," but "when?" While it would be presumptuous to predict the time of the passing of mall life (one cannot at this point even predict the success or failure of any particular mall with any certainty—let alone the extinction of all malls), it might be useful to speculate on what might replace mall life upon its passing.

With this in mind, let's outline some of the things mall life provides for its participants. First and foremost, it offers a way for many people to contend with boredom by offering entertainment or just plain diversion. Second, it provides convenient shopping. Third, it offers safe free "public" social space—a way to meet and interact with others (an indoor street corner society).

What other set of circumstances and/or contrivances could provide the same (or similar) conditions and at the same time compete with existing mall life? One possible answer is a combination of T.V., video games, and computers. Take for example, a major mall function of providing convenient shopping. If the emphasis was on convenience, one could shop at home for most things by having the stock of Sears Department store displayed by name, price, and in color upon one's T.V. screen. Having found what you wanted, you would then punch your credit card and item number into the computer. The item would be charged to your credit card account and delivered to your home within a day or two, in much the same manner as one can now phone up for the home delivery of a pizza or a "belly-gram." Certainly this would be convenient. You would never again have to leave the comfort of safety of your living room, find the shopping mall, a place to park, the store you sought, wait in line to pay, or negotiate your way out of the mall and back home.

On a small scale this service is already available. One sees record albums, luggage, log splitters, "oriental cookers," "Samurai" kitchen knives, and wonder wheel barrels for sale on T.V. Just lift your phone and call the toll-free number, give your credit card number, "and allow four to six weeks for delivery." If one cannot defer gratification for four to six weeks, a more current version of the T.V. shopper was noted in a recent newspaper article entitled, "Now, Direct from Cattle Country, Heifers and Bulls for Sale on T.V." (Padilla, 1982).

> Small but growing numbers of auctions are being held in hotels, when an auctioneer peddles the beef via 50-inch screens, beaming color video tapes of cattle herds roaming in their natural setting. Perspective buyers, properly attired in Sunday boots and hats, shout their bids between sips of cocktails.

This is closer to what the author has suggested above. It also overcomes the alienating effect of watching T.V. alone, that is, one gets together with others in their homes for an on-the-spot shopping trip and social get-together — something between a coffee clutch and a Tupperware party. I would expect that with the expansion of cable television, home computers, and video games, video shopping would be a natural extension.

Television has in just a few years generated new markets and cut into old ones in ways no one imagined. For example, the current proliferation of video games has put a big dent in the teenage record and cassette business (Grover, 1982). Teenagers who are now spending more money on video games are spending less on phonograph records and audio cassettes. This is, of course, a natural extension of the "T.V. generation." Pop music can now be had on cable T.V. and not only listened to, but watched. This phenomenon has cut into Hi-Fi sales (a big teenage market); and some think, has contributed to the slump in book sales as well.

Given that most of the current buying market is composed of people who grew up with T.V. as a way of life, the expansion of shopping and socializing by T.V. is probably a good bet. Should this become sufficiently popular, it might well contribute to a significant reduction in shopping mall popularity, or in the longer run, its demise.

References

"Antitrust Action in Shopping Malls." 1975, *Business Week,* No. 2410, December 8, p. 51.

Arehart, Teichel, Joan. 1979, "Can the Barrier Beaches Be Saved". *Science News,* January 6, V. 115, N1, p. 10 (3).

Baird, George and Sampson, Barry. 1981, "Main Street: Can it Survive the Shopping Center?". *City Magazine,* V. 5, N1, p. 32 (14).

"Bankruptcy Courts Struggle to Cope with Growing Caseload." 1982, *The Wall Street Journal,* Thursday, May 6, p. 1.

Barmash, Isadore. 1982, "Buying a Piece of a Shopping Center." *The New York Times,* Sunday, April 18, p. 14f.

Bleda, Paul R. and Bleda, Sharon E. 1978, "Effects of Sex and Smoking on Reactions to Spatial Invasion at a Shopping Mall." *Journal of Social Psychology,* April, V. 104 (2).

Blustein, Paul. 1982, "Is the Stock Market Really Efficient? Go Ask a Bubba". *The Wall Street Journal,* March 15, p. 1.

Brownell, Kelly, D., et al. 1980, "Evaluation and Modification of Exercise Patterns in the Natural Environment." *American Journal of Psychiatry,* December, V. 137 (12).

"Bugged". 1982, *Syracuse New Times,* June 9, p. 5.

Carbone, James. 1982, "Video Arcade Dispute Heating Up". *Syracuse Herald-American,* Sunday, May 9, p. B1.

Carpenter, Horace. 1978, *Shopping Center Management.* New York, N.Y.: International Council of Shopping Centers.

Emerson, Joan. 1969, "Nothing Unusual is Happening". paper read at the September Annual Meeting of the American Sociological Association.

Feagin, Joe. 1982, *Building Capitalist Cities: Developers, Bankers, Consumers.* Englewood Cliffs, N.J.: Prentice-Hall (forthcoming).

Getlin, Josh. 1982, "$100-Million Beverly Center, 'Blessing and Curse', Opens". *Los Angeles Times,* Thursday, February 4, p. 1, part IX.

Goffman, Erving. 1959, *The Presentation of Self in Everyday Life.* Garden City, N.Y.: Doubleday & Company, Inc.

Green, Alan. 1978, "The Battle of Pyramid Mall." *Environmental Action,* November 4, V. 10, N13, p. 4 (4).

Grover, Stephen. 1982, "Record Business Slumps as Taping and Video Games Take Away Sales". *The Wall Street Journal,* Thursday, February 18, p. 31.

Gruen, Victor. 1973, *Centers for the Urban Environment: Survival of the Cities.* New York, N.Y.: Van Nostrand Reinhold Company.

Harris, Bruce, et al. 1978, "Density and Personal Space in a Field Setting." *Social Psychology Quarterly,* December, Vol. 41 (4).

Ircha, Michael C. 1981, "Regulating Shopping Centers: Canadian and International Experience". *City Magazine,* V. 5, N1, p. 68 (9).

Jacobs, Jerry. 1974 (1983 reprint), *Fun City: An Ethnographic Study of a Retirement Community.* Prospect Heights, Illinois: Waveland Press, Inc.

Jacobs, Sanford L. 1982, "How to Prevent an Employee from Ripping Off the Firm." *The Wall Street Journal,* Monday, May 10, p. 33.

King, R. 1976, "A Frightening Job Loss in a 'City Built of Fear'". *Business Week,* No. 2420, February 23, p. 18 R-T.

Lang, Craeme. 1981, "Shopping Centers: The Case Study of Corner Brook." *City Magazine,* V. 5, N1, p. 46 (16).

Lawson, H. et al. 1974, "Nottingham Refuse Incineration and District Heating Scheme." (Survey Report) *Inst. Civil Engineers Proc.,* April, V. 56, p. 11 (19).

"Lewisham Shopping Centre Opened." 1977, *Director, The,* Vol. 29, No. 9, March, p. 30.

Liebow, Elliot. 1967, *Tally's Corner,* Boston: Mass.: Little Brown & Co.

Pfuhl, Edwin, Jr. 1980, *The Deviance Process.* New York: D. Van Nostrand Co.

"Shopping Habits...Screening Tenants...Top U.S. Buildings." 1982, *Wall Street Journal,* April 21, p. 31.

"Signing Can Program the Customer Through the Mall." 1973, *Chain Store Age,* (Exec. Ed.) 49 (Aug.): 30, 32, 34.

Simmel, Georg. 1950, "The Metropolis and Mental Life" in Kurt H. Wolff, editor and translator, *The Sociology of Georg Simmel.* New York: The Free Press.

Teschler, L. 1980, "Setting Sail for the Virgin Islands." *Industrial Week,* Vol. 204, No. 4, February 18, pp. 77-80.

United States Department of Labor Training Report of the President. 1979, Tables A-3 and A-22; and Bureau of Labor Statistics, Unpublished, 1979 data.

"When Lenders Share Homebuyer Equity". 1980, *Business Week,* No. 2658, October 13, pp. 45-46.

Whyte, William Foote. 1943, *Street Corner Society.* Chicago, Ill.: The University of Chicago Press.

Chapter 2

Architects, Developers and Contractors
Designing and Building Malls

Having dealt in the first chapter with a general introduction to shopping malls, we will now go on to take up in some detail the conception of the mall from the architect's perspective. What sorts of considerations does the architect entertain and in what sequence in order for a mall to materialize? Actually, there are many preliminary steps that must be taken before the architect can begin to conceptualize the mall proper (Redstone, 1973*; Birakrant, M. 1970).

Preliminary Considerations: Feasibility Studies

First demographic studies must reveal that a market exists in the targeted area, i.e., that there are sufficient numbers of persons of the right age and income within a certain number of miles of the mall to provide potential customers. Next, traffic studies are made to establish if there are any potential traffic problems. Soil test, zoning restrictions, financial resources and the availability of reasonable financing are other factors that must also be taken into account. Above all else the cost of development must not be prohibitive. If none of these present a serious problem, the project moves on to the design phase.

Design Phase

In this stage of development, the architect begins to make some preliminary decisions regarding the general design of the mall. These include such items as how large the mall is to be (its Gross Leasable Area), how many stores (how broad a base to spread the expense over), how many levels, how

---

*Much of the following discussion is based upon the work of Louis G. Redstone in a book entitled, *New Dimensions in Shopping Centers and Stores,* New York: McGraw-Hill & Co., 1973.

many "anchors," parking for how many cars, and interior and entrance and exit roads.

When these and other considerations have been assessed, schematic design drawings are made to illustrate the scale of the project, the basic structure, the materials to be used and services the mall will offer. This is followed by preliminary cost estimates and approvals by the owners for going ahead with the project. If everything is found to be feasible and agreeable to all concerned at this stage of the process, floor plans are drawn and leasing documents are prepared. Apart from considerations of general layout, the floor plans are used to show prospective tenants the location and dimensions of the space they will be leasing, discuss the utilities and other mall services, as well as the sales prospects the architect and owners envision.

Concurrent with these happenings, models of the mall are exhibited along with drawings to illustrate to the owners (and would be tenants) the mall's planned interior and exterior design. In this regard the leasing agent accentuates the positive and tries to eliminate the negative, in an effort to get the most concessions from the prospective tenant. Having involved a sufficient number of committed tenants the project moves on to the design development phase.

During this stage a more detailed rendering of the mall proper and site plans in general are drawn based upon earlier schematic design drawings. Decisions are reached on the sorts of systems needed to operationalize mechanical, electrical and other mall services. More detailed consideration is also given to the many other aspects of the mall's requirements noted earlier. Following this stage of development, the work progresses from the design to the production phase. Architect consultants are hired to take care of the various engineering services involved in the project. The developer begins to delegate greater responsibility to lower eschelon persons in the hierarchy to take care of the day to day problems of preparing project documents as well as dealing with leasing questions. A "tenant coordinator" is usually put in charge of this aspect of the operation. This individual has a direct line of communication to the architect who supplies him with any necessary information about leasing requirements.

Documentation and Structuring the Work

The actual construction of the mall is usually undertaken in one of two ways. The first and more conventional way, is to prepare complete construction documents for the entire project. At this point bids for the work are taken and negotiations are initiated for a lump-sum commitment to cover the cost of the project. On the basis of this commitment, financing is arranged and construction contracts are let with the contractors. In the second form, the project is constructed in stages. This form of multistage bidding for the scheduled construction of various aspects of the work is called "overlapping," "staggered," or "fast-track" scheduling. The latter arrangement is believed by some to provide a savings in construction time, and sometimes costs.

Finally, with the financing arranged and the bids on construction costs in, the project enters the next stage of development, i.e., the selection of contractors who will actually undertake the mall's construction.

Selecting Contractors

There are two basic ways of selecting contractors, (1) competitive bidding or (2) direct selection and negotiation. The guidelines for the first form of contractor selection and what the mall owner and contractor have a right to expect of each other during these negotiations is set forth in an AIA document entitled, *Recommended Guide for Bidding Procedures and Contract Award.* The following excerpt gives a good summary of these reciprocal expectations.

> The Owner certainly has the right to expect that the Architect has exercised due diligence and skill in the preparation of the Contract Documents, and that these documents adequately describe the completed building to the Contractor, who can then provide such a building, certainly adequate for its intended purpose.

> The Contractor has a right to expect that information on the Contract Documents is sufficient to enable him to prepare complete estimates, and that the Architect is familiar with the local ordinances relating to the design and construction of buildings in that particular area. Unusual stipulations required by local authorities should be completely described in the construction documents.

> The Architect, on the other hand, has the right to expect full confidence from the Owner during the bidding procedure particularly in connection with recommendation and selection of bidders, and the actual receipt of bids.

> Finally, all parties have a right to expect complete cooperation from the other parties to the process, as well as an ultimate contract award in line with accepted procedures and practices outlined in the documents, free from unwarranted negotiation or price cutting by Owner, Architect, or the low bidder's competitors.

In general, competitive bidding usually results in contract awards based upon lump sum forms of bidding (noted earlier), while the direct selection and negotiation form of awarding contracts, is usually associated with "...either the cost of work plus a lump sum, or percentage fee, with the former more in evidence" (Redstone, 1973).

Construction Manager

There is in all of these complex arrangements sometimes a "middle man" between the architect, owners and contractors. This individual is called the "construction manager" and represents the owners. His job has a number of facets. For one thing he is the liaison person who provides the architect with feedback during the design and construction document phases. This enables the architect to select materials of the proper "...quality, durability, finish, appearance (and) maintainability" (Redstone, 1973). The construction manager is also required to provide the architect with accurate cost data information while the project is under construction in order to keep the total completed costs of the mall close to the original estimates.

Sometimes the construction manager is given such broad responsibilities for maintaining quality control and reasonable expenditures, that when things go wrong, the owner (who the construction manager represents) is held responsible, not the contractor. In other cases, the responsibilities of the construction manager are more narrowly defined and he is responsible only for coordinating the project, watching over quality control, changes in the work schedule, and the approval of payments.

Scheduling

When the mall construction is to begin and be completed is of crucial concern to the owners and tenants. For example, if the project were completed after December, the three month period that constitutes "the Christmas season" would have expired, and with it 50% or more of all annual sales. Nearly everyone has a vested interest in getting the job done on schedule. In order to insure that it is, the construction manager must have some way to monitor how much work has been completed and how much is left to complete. In this undertaking he usually invokes two major systems of analysis — PERT and CPM.

PERT is an abbreviation for "Program Evaluation and Review Technique" and is designed to provide a way of establishing whether or not work scheduled for completion by a certain date has in fact been completed. CPM ("Critical Path Method") is a form of analysis designed to monitor and review how much work remains to be done, as opposed to how much has already been completed. In terms of monitoring construction activities and progress, CPM is probably the more useful when properly applied. It is a graphic method of preplanning which depicts in detail how much work has yet to be completed, and projects a completion date for each stage of the construction work. A diagram (Redstone, 1973) is given on page twenty-four to help the reader envision this procedure.

Of course, in the construction business, as in the retail business, all is not science, and even elegant monitoring devices such as PERT and CPM sometimes fall to the effects of random occurrences such as strikes, the weather, delayed deliveries of material and the ready availability of manpower. If such devices are no guarantee that the mall is completed on schedule, they are useful tools to help monitor and guide such an undertaking.

The Construction Phase

There are within the stages of mall development considered thus far, three major figures. The developer, the architect and the contractor. Each has certain obligations to the other during the construction phase if the project is to be completed on time and within the budget.

For example, the developer must provide all vital information regarding the tenants' needs as these relate to construction. They must also be careful not to let separate site contracts e.g., sidewalk, parking lot or landscaping projects, that will be ill-timed and interfere with the construction of the mall proper. The developer should also decide whether or not there will be one or more major contractors who will build the mall and the stores. If there are two or more separate contractors, one for the mall and another for the stores, a good deal of coordination is required, not only so that one does not get in the other's way, but so that if one falls behind in some way, it does not disrupt the efforts of the other. As noted earlier, the developer relies on the construction manager to coordinate these efforts. When the project is well underway a second person, the "chief engineer," sometimes assists in these efforts. The architect is obliged to assist the developer and his representatives (the construction manager and chief engineer) in making sure the project is well coordinated and going ahead on schedule and within the budget. In order to monitor the construction and maximize coordination by minimizing last minute changes, the developer and architect must pay special attention to "tenant-induced changes" to the mall shell. These, it turns out, are both most numerous and costly. The following are some examples (Redstone, 1973).

> Revisions to the size and type of neutral piers
> Addition of floor depressions or raised floor areas
> The necessity of roof openings for the venting of HVAC equipment or toilet exhausts
> Addition of conduit and piping within dividing walls or above ceilings in shell spaces

Diagram Showing Theoretical Path Method

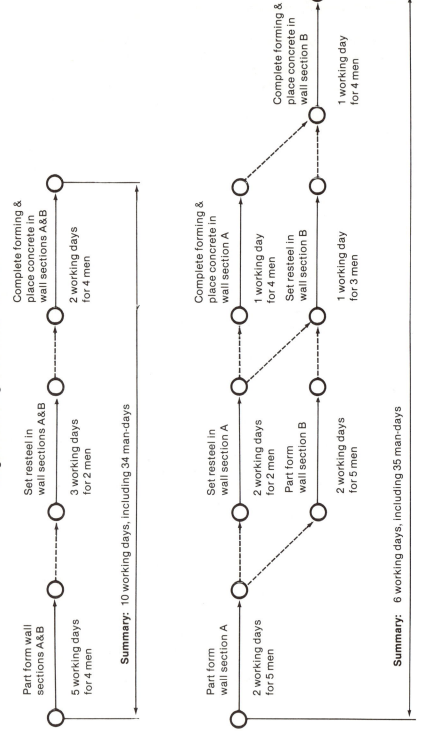

Part form wall sections A&B

5 working days for 4 men

Set resteel in wall sections A&B

3 working days for 2 men

Complete forming & place concrete in wall sections A&B

2 working days for 4 men

Summary: 10 working days, including 34 man-days

Part form wall section A

2 working days for 5 men

Set resteel in wall section A

2 working days for 2 men

Complete forming & place concrete in wall section A

1 working day for 4 men

Part form wall section B

2 working days for 5 men

Set resteel in wall section B

1 working day for 3 men

Complete forming & place concrete in wall section B

1 working day for 4 men

Summary: 6 working days, including 35 man-days

Additional electrical loadings added to the basic loads designed into the project

The addition of specially insulated spaces or spaces having special security requirements

Unusual heating, cooling, or ventilation requirements

The addition of storage or selling mezzanines

Extra heavy loadings at the storefront line to accommodate the storefront itself

Signing or other tenant facilities

Special roof loadings for roof-hung equipment

Special provision for receipt of tenant deliveries and/or removal of tenant wastes

The relocation of exit signs (which always seem to be required by the fire marshal in a location different from that shown on the drawings!)

"Interferences" between tenant and center piping, ductwork, structure, and so forth

The developer is usually obliged to accommodate the tenant in making unanticipated revisions of this sort. While such changes cannot be totally anticipated or eliminated, their cost and inconvenience may be minimized if they are recognized early in the construction process.

Another key person in the coordination process is the "tenant coordinator" (noted earlier in the chapter). He or she is in charge of monitoring the progress and quality of construction work as it relates to the tenants' best interests. If the work done by the contractor for the tenant is not up to the caliber outlined in the lease documents, the tenant coordinator's job is to launch a protest early in the process and see that the problem is corrected. Tenant related problems dealing with the construction of tenant spaces frequently take one of the following forms (Redstone, 1973):

problems related to utilities
prorating costs of interferences
cleanup charges
fire protection
debris removal
coordination of roof cutting
patching or
traffic

Completion and Occupancy

When all that has been outlined above has been accomplished and the mall and tenant spaces have been completed (along with the outside parking spaces, on site roads, landscaping, and outside lighting) the mall is ready for occupancy. At this stage the developer initiates the "guarantee period" with the contractor (upon completion of construction), completes his final financing agreements, and "resolves all tenant allowances against actual costs of building the tenant spaces" (Redstone, 1973).

Finally the architect and contractor assist during this concluding stage by resolving any grievances between themselves and/or with the owner or tenants. With the resolution of these differences the mall is ready for occupancy. Some of the basic configurations that completed malls take are given below and on subsequent pages (Carpenter, 1978).

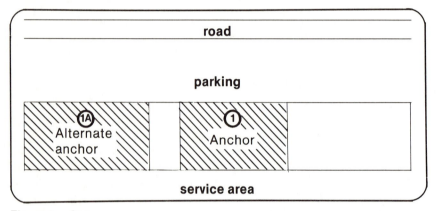

Figure 1 — Strip

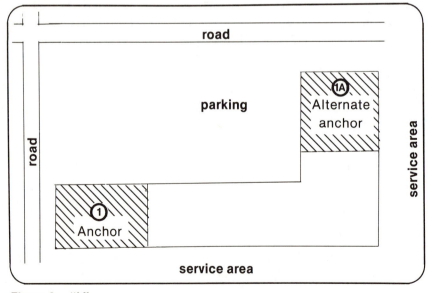

Figure 2 — "L"

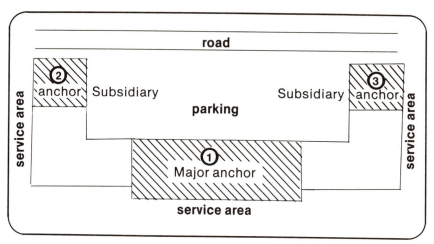

Figure 3 — "U"

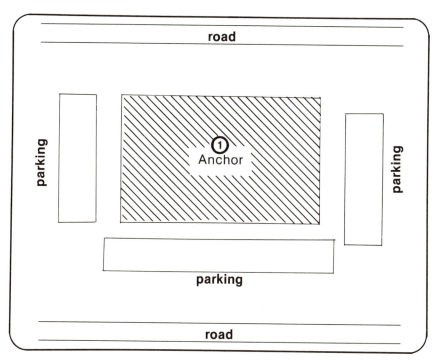

Figure 4 — Cluster

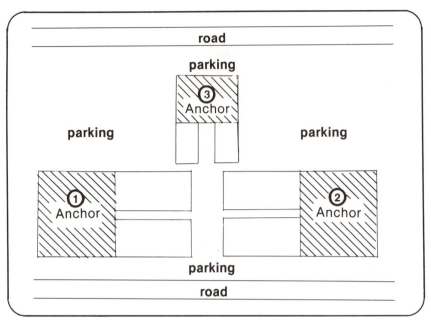

Figure 5 — "T"

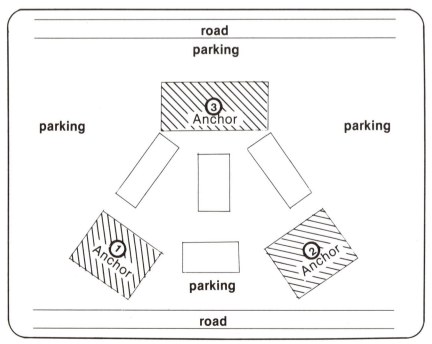

Figure 6 — Triangle

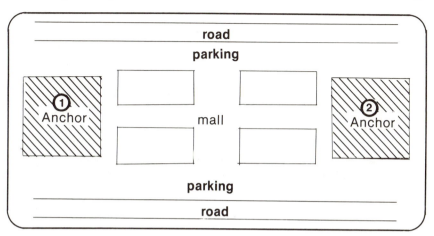

Figure 7 — Dumbell

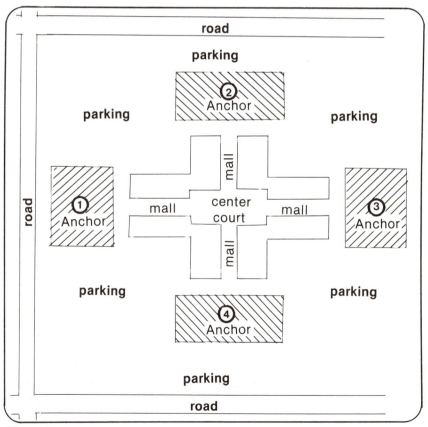

Figure 8 — Double Dumbbell

What to Plan For

The above is an idealized outline of the relationship of the architect, developer and contractor and their duties and mutual obligations toward one another during the various design and construction stages of the mall. I say idealized version because on the mall (as in the world at large) all does not always go according to plan. The initial construction estimates and finished costs may be miles apart; completion date estimates may not be met; architect fees (usually determined on a percent of the total cost of the project) may go up as the cost of the project unexpectedly escalates; and the quality of workmanship may be deemed by the owners to be sub-standard. These and numerous other considerations may erupt before, during, or after completion of the project and result in lengthy legal battles. For example, a Beverly Hills Mall is now involved in expensive litigation on these and other issues (Hiltzik, 1982).

> Millions of dollars' worth of construction disputes are marring the debut of Rodeo Collection, a chic five-story shopping center in Beverly Hills.
>
> Since the $35-million project on Rodeo Drive opened more than a month ago, shoppers have wandered about its extravagantly marbled central court and through the handful of elegant shops already open. But in the same period more than 16 contractors have filed claims against the developers for unpaid bills that now total more than $3.1 million.
>
> Contractors in virtually every construction trade, from glazing to plumbing, have filed mechanic's liens against the Collection's owners...
>
> Daryoush Mahboubi Fardi, the project's Iranian-born general partner, says many of the disagreements result from what he says are his uniquely exacting standards for the workmanship on his building...
>
> There is no dispute that Rodeo Collection presented unusual challenges for engineers and builders...
>
> Meeting such challenges helped drive the project's construction costs well over the initial estimates to $22 million, Mahboubi says, from $16 million. Along with design and land expenses, the center cost about $35 million, or four to five times as much per square foot as conventional shopping malls in the region.

Notwithstanding these and other problems, the idealized version presented earlier offers a reasonable scenario on how it is "supposed to go," even if in the real world, it sometimes goes otherwise. With this disclaimer on record, we have shown in the abstract how the design and construction of shopping malls is undertaken and seen through to completion. What we have not discussed in any detail is the variation in tenant mix in different size shopping centers (or different classes of centers) and how this is intimately related to the sorts of tenant spaces the architect must plan for. The question of tenant mix was mentioned earlier in other contexts, e.g., in regard to the large proportion of women's wear stores. However, it has not yet been given a very detailed treatment, especially as it relates to architectural and design concerns and the ultimate flavor of the mall. What sorts of tenants do the four different size malls (super regional, regional, community, and neighborhood) contain and how do architects plan for these differences? To deal with the first part of this question first we present below segments of four tables (Dollars and Cents of Shopping Center: 1981) which list for each of these kinds of malls 20 different kinds of tenants and their percentage of GLA and sales.

Table 1

**Super Regional Shopping Centers:
Composition by Tenant Classification Group**

	Percent GLA Mall Shops	Percent Sales
General merchandise (excluding department stores)	12.7	8.1
Food	8.9	18.1
Food services	6.9	7.0
Clothing	23.7	25.7
Shoes	6.3	7.4
Home furnishings	2.2	1.5
Home appliances/music	3.3	4.6
Building materials/garden	1.8	1.3
Automotive supplies/service station	1.5	.5
Hobby/special interest	3.4	3.8
Gifts/specialty	4.5	4.6
Jewelry and cosmetics	2.3	5.2
Liquor	.5	.3
Drugs	3.7	4.8
Other retail	3.0	2.1
Personal services	2.1	1.9
Recreation/community	5.2	1.6
Financial	2.6	.4
Offices (other than financial)	2.2	.5
Other	3.2	.6
Total	100.0	100.0

Table 2
Regional Shopping Centers:
Composition by Tenant Classification Group

	Percent GLA	Percent Sales
General merchandise	35.4	25.6
Food	14.9	34.3
Food services	4.7	4.5
Clothing	7.4	7.1
Shoes	2.0	1.8
Home furnishings	2.5	1.4
Home appliances/music	1.8	1.8
Building materials/garden	2.2	1.6
Automotive supplies/service station	2.1	1.2
Hobby, special interest	2.2	1.9
Gifts/specialty	2.1	1.5
Jewelry and cosmetics	.8	1.5
Liquor	.6	.4
Drugs	4.6	5.9
Other retail	2.8	1.6
Personal services	2.5	1.1
Recreation/community	3.3	.8
Financial	3.0	5.4
Offices (other than financial)	2.1	.2
Other	3.0	.4
Total	100.0	100.0

Table 3
Community Shopping Centers:
Composition by Tenant Classification Group

	Percent GLA	Percent Sales
General merchandise	6.6	3.6
Food	27.8	57.9
Food services	8.6	6.5
Clothing	5.3	5.1
Shoes	1.1	.8
Home furnishings	2.2	.8
Home appliances/music	2.0	1.2
Building materials/garden	3.1	1.3
Automotive supplies/service station	2.4	1.1
Hobby, special interest	2.6	1.8
Gifts/specialty	2.6	1.7
Jewelry and cosmetics	.6	.7
Liquor	1.5	2.0
Drugs	9.3	9.9
Other retail	3.5	1.5
Personal services	5.4	2.1
Recreation/community	3.4	.7
Financial	4.3	.1
Offices (other than financial)	3.2	.7
Other	4.5	.5
Total	100.0	100.0

Table 4

Neighborhood Shopping Centers:
Composition by Tenant Classification Group

	Percent GLA Mall Shops	Percent Sales
General merchandise (excluding department stores)	15.1	10.0
Food	14.2	27.3
Food services	7.0	6.7
Clothing	16.6	18.6
Shoes	4.4	5.5
Home furnishings	2.4	1.5
Home appliances/music	2.8	3.5
Building materials/garden	2.0	1.2
Automotive supplies/service station	1.9	.8
Hobby/special interest	3.1	3.2
Gifts/specialty	3.8	3.7
Jewelry and cosmetics	1.6	3.8
Liquor	.7	.6
Drugs	4.9	5.6
Other retail	3.2	2.1
Personal services	2.8	1.6
Recreation/community	4.3	1.3
Financial	3.5	2.2
Offices (other than financial)	2.4	.5
Other	3.3	.3
Total	100.0	100.0

We can see from these tables that depending upon the size of the mall, the exterior and interior design will vary with the tenant mix. For example, on super regional and regional size malls, clothing and general merchandise comprise nearly as much GLA as all of the remaining categories of tenants combined. This statistic is accentuated when we realize that the figures for clothing and general merchandise in the tables above do not include the malls "anchors" or department stores. On the other hand, in community shopping centers general merchandise and food comprise by far the greatest percent of GLA, and in neighborhood centers the two greatest consumers of GLA are food and food services. The above statistics bear directly upon what the architect is asked to plan for in building a shopping mall. They also have a good deal to do with the tenants' planning of what size mall to become a part of, depending upon the past performance of the businesses he has in mind. For example, we can see that while clothing and food are the two businesses with the highest percentage of sales on regional and super regional malls, food and general merchandise are highest on community malls, and food and drugs on the neighborhood malls.

While the question of tenant mix has been shown to be in part a function of the size of the shopping center, and an important factor in everyone's equation (the architect, potential tenant and mall management) the statistics noted above (and thousands of others) have only recently become available. You may remember from Chapter 1 how very wrong the economist's projections were regarding the business volume of one of the early malls constructed in the 1950's. The reason given was that the economist had little or no prior data on which to base future projections accurately. This was true not only of economists but anthropologists and sociologists who conducted early studies of suburban shopping mall potential. One example is a study of *The Shopping Center Versus Downtown* (Jonassen, 1955). This work was a demographic and survey research study of the motivation, shopping habits, and attitudes of suburban and urban shoppers in three cities: Columbus, Ohio; Seattle, Washington; and Houston, Texas. Studies of this kind were then, and are now, common place. As indicated at the beginning of this chapter they are seen by the architect and developer as a necessary first step in establishing whether or not there is a local market, i.e., an adequate pool of appropriate consumers, and the economic and class characteristics of these persons. Given the importance of such studies, in what ways did early social science researchers go wrong in anticipating *what* to study? How did these errors in judgement affect their recommendations to developers and architects, and the future design and social life of malls?

Let's consider the study noted above with respect to what was studied and what was not and why the researcher chose to look at what he did. As indicated throughout, the main motivation of mall developers, tenants and management, is the profit motive. When owners hire various experts to study the demographic, attitudinal or economic features of social life, they do so in order to get the sort of information that is necessary for them to make a series of rational decisions on how to maximize profits over the short and long run. Sociological studies have reflected this central concern of research consumers. First and foremost you want to find out how many potential customers there are, how much money they have to spend, how to get them to come to the mall, and ultimately how to get them to spend the money they have while they are there. All of these concerns revolve around the central notion of the would be mall customer as consumer. As such, it would seem reasonable (both to the researcher and the consumers of the research) to get the answers to questions that have to do with the potential customers' shopping habits and what will be likely to draw him or her to the mall (as opposed to the other possible shopping areas). Such questions usually deal with safety, cleanliness, ease of access and parking, good shopping value, status, convenience and so on. Again, all of this deals directly or indirectly with the respondent as consumer. An example of this, from Jonassens study (1955), are some of the questions that shoppers were asked in order to construct "Shopping Attitudes Scale II."

Shopping Attitude Scale II

46 One of the things I like about shopping downtown is the good delivery service.

strongly agree	agree	undecided	disagree	strongly disagree
5	4	3	2	1

47 One of the things I like about downtown is the ease with which I can establish a charge account.

strongly agree	agree	undecided	disagree	strongly disagree
5	4	3	2	1

48 It is easier to return and exchange goods in the suburban shopping center than downtown.

strongly agree	agree	undecided	disagree	strongly disagree
1	2	3	4	5

49 One of the things I like about suburban shopping is that it is so much easier to take children shopping there.

strongly agree	agree	undecided	disagree	strongly disagree
1	2	3	4	5

50 I find a better quality of goods in the suburban shopping center.

strongly agree	agree	undecided	disagree	strongly disagree
1	2	3	4	5

51 When comparing downtown and suburban stores, I find the prices lower for the same quality of goods in suburban shopping centers.

strongly agree	agree	undecided	disagree	strongly disagree
1	2	3	4	5

52 Downtown is a good place to combine different kinds of shopping and other things I may want to do.

strongly agree	agree	undecided	disagree	strongly disagree
5	4	3	2	1

53 When shopping downtown, I find the amount of walking required is altogether too much.

strongly agree	agree	undecided	disagree	strongly disagree
1	2	3	4	5

54   I find that the suburban stores generally give a more dependable guarantee of goods.

strongly agree	agree	undecided	disagree	strongly disagree
1	2	3	4	5

55   Stores in the suburban shopping center keep more convenient hours.

strongly agree	agree	undecided	disagree	strongly disagree
1	2	3	4	5

56   One of the things I like about the suburban shopping center is the comparative peace and quiet and lack of crowding and dirt.

strongly agree	agree	undecided	disagree	strongly disagree
1	2	3	4	5

57   When I want to go shopping downtown for such things as clothing and furniture, the time it takes me matters:

very much	much	some	a little	not at all
1	2	3	4	5

58   As far as I am concerned, the cost of transportation to downtown matters:

very much	much	some	a little	not at all
1	2	3	4	5

59   When I go shopping for clothing, I:

always go downtown	usually go downtown	am undecided	usually go to the SSC	always go to the SSC
5	4	3	2	1

60   When I go shopping for furniture and household furnishings, I:

always go downtown	usually go downtown	am undecided	usually go to the SSC	always go to the SSC
5	4	3	2	1

What we find in these questions and those associated with other studies (Bearden, 1977; Goldman, 1976; Martineau, 1958) is what we would expect to find given the questions that the researcher (and the consumers to the research) hope to answer. These questions, apart from their varying content, will deal in one way or another with, Who's out there? How much money do they have to spend? What would they like to buy? How can we get them to like and buy the merchandise we have to sell (Jacobs, 1979)? And how do we get them to buy it here?

Conspicuously absent are questions that might be concerned with potential customers not as economic consumers, but as consumers of free entertainment, leisure-time activities, a therapeutic, safe, or comfortable environment, or someone in search of a setting for "time out" activites and a respite from the rigors and/or boredom of everyday life. In short, the potential customer is addressed as economic, and not social man. Such an overly pragmatic and myopic view has (to mix a metaphor or two) produced serious oversights. This book will argue that many (perhaps most mall customers) do not frequent the mall for economic, but rather for social and social psychological reasons.

Some of the general findings of the mid 1950's study noted above are interesting as they relate to Columbus, Ohio (Jonassen, 1955). For example, it was found that: The higher educational classes, higher income groups, persons having urban or metropolitan backgrounds, and those who were females indicated higher satisfaction with downtown shopping than did persons of lower income, less education, or rural background, and of the male sex.

It is probably the case that today these findings would be closer to the truth if rotated 180 degrees. Persons with higher income, education and formally metropolitans, would most likely now be suburbanites, and favor shopping at suburban malls. Persons of rural backgrounds, lower income and education and male (or female) would more likely live in the inner city and rarely shop at suburban malls. Allowing that early researchers overlooked the social significance of malls (for the reasons noted above) and that they could not have been expected to recognize the fantastic growth in the number or influence of malls upon the nation's social life, more recent studies cannot make that claim. Current researchers have had the benefit of hindsight, and should by now be cognizant of the vast institutional importance of shopping malls and how they have rewoven the social fabric of suburban and urban life.

Some professionals have in various contexts, of course, come to this recognition. For example, in a lawsuit brought by the National Organization for Women (NOW) against the Westfarms Mall in Farmington, Connecticut, their attorney Martin Margulies maintained that "*...malls are the place, the only place, to see people in the suburbs anymore*" (Emphasis Added). The dispute between NOW and the mall owners turned upon whether or not the mall is public domain. If it is, the distribution of political literature is acceptable, if not, the mall management may prohibit it (Geist, 1983).

Not withstanding the considerable number of newspaper and magazine articles devoted to the expanding social significance of malls, and the expansion of trade books and articles on various pragmatic issues dealing with the operation, design or development of malls, there is not to my knowledge (at the time of this writing) a single social science *book* devoted to the social life of shopping malls, or the significance of the expanded growth and use of malls upon the larger society. The author is amazed to find that this book, if it is not the only one on the topic, is certainly one of a very few.*

We have dealt in this chapter with the reciprocal duties and obligations of architects, contractors and owners. The construction and operation of malls is undertaken with one overriding goal in mind—showing a profit. Outlined in this chapter (from a variety of viewpoints) are the kinds and sources of information that architects, contractors, and owners need in order to succeed in such an undertaking. It is not just engineers, architects, realtor or financiers who are needed if one is to succeed in the mall business. Social science consultants such as demographers, survey researchers, qualitative sociologists, and economists are all essential not only for establishing the initial feasibility of a mall project, but for monitoring its ongoing course. The latter measure is as necessary as the former, since as every social scientist knows, if "change is inevitable," its direction is not.

References

Bearden, W.O. 1977, "Determinant Attributes of Store Patronage: Downtown Versus Outlying Shopping Centers." *Journal of Retailing,* 53 (2): 15-22.

Birnkrant, M. 1970, "Shopping Center Feasibility Study: Its Methods and Techniques." *Journal of Property Management,* 35, 272-279.

Carpenter, Horace. 1978, *Shopping Center Management.* New York, NY: International Council of Shopping Centers.

Dollars and Cents of Shopping Centers. 1981, Washington, D.C.: Urban Land Institute.

Glist, William E. 1983, "Shopping Malls Protest Intrusion by Protesters." *New York Times,* Tuesday, July 7, p. B1.

Goldman, A. 1976, "Do Lower-Income Customers Have a More Restricted Shopping Scope?" *Journal of Marketing,* 40 (1): 46-54.

Hiltzik, Michael A. 1982, "Contractors, Owners in Flap Over Paying for Mall." *Los Angeles Times,* Friday, December 31, p. 1, part 4.

Jonassen, C.T. 1955, *The Shopping Center Versus Downtown.* Columbus, Ohio: Bureau of Business Research, College of Commerce and Administration, The Ohio State University.

Martineau, P. 1958, "Social Classes and Spending Behavior." *Journal of Marketing,* 23 (October): 121-130.

Redstone, Louis. 1973, *New Dimensions in Shopping Centers and Stores.* New York: McGraw-Hill and Co.

*This contention is based upon a review of one major survey of the literature, James F. Orr, *Malls, Pedestrian Malls, and Shopping Centers: A Selected Bibliography with Annotations,* Monticello, Illinois: Vance Bibliographies, 1979; the author's more current readings, and the contention of a number of large book store owners that such a work is currently unavailable.

Errata for Jacobs, *The Mall: An Attempted Escape from Everyday Life*

These typographical errors have been brought to our attention; they will be corrected in subsequent printings of *The Mall.*

Page 4   Line 28 "provided at the back of the book" should read "provided at the end of each chapter."

Page 49   Line 9 "Table 1" should read "Table 3."

Line 29 "This is consistent with..." should be the last sentence in the previous paragraph.

Page 62   Line 8 "extend" should read "extent."

Page 103   Line 2, the first "to" should read "go."

Line 27 through 30 are incorrect lines. The first four lines of this paragraph should read as follows:

There are other routine forms of shopping that also help to bring suburban housewives to the mall. Some malls (the Spendville Mall, for example) incorporate a supermarket. Women doing their grocery shopping rarely pass up an opportunity to frequent the mall proper. The library, post...

Page 112   Line 26 "escpae" should read "escape."

Chapter Three

The Organizational and Economic
Structure of Malls

Formal Organization

Not infrequently, shopping malls located in the same geographical area are owned and operated by the same developer, but organized under different legal entities. For example, in Oldtown, Eagan Associates owns and manages a number of malls each of which are organized as separate legal entities and under different names.

Overseeing mall business is the mall manager. He or she usually has a private secretary, while a second secretary covers any business associated with the Merchant's Association (a sub-set of the mall organization we will consider in greater detail below). Also, assisting the manager is a file clerk, bookkeeper, salesperson, leasing representative, a person in charge of collecting monthly gross sales figures, an accountant, a marketing director, a computer programmer, and a head of security. Some of these employees, e.g., the bookkeeper, accountant, salesperson and computer programmer, assist not only the Shoptime manager, but the managers of the two other malls owned by Eagan as well. This does not include 15 part-time security persons, or the "farmed out" task of mall maintenance.

In addition to being responsible for mall security, maintenance, collecting rent, collecting sales figures, insurance problems, dealing with tenants, the media, marketing, advertising, and the mall budget, the mall manager must also deal with the greater outside community. As the Shoptime manager put it, "It's basically like a small city and you're in charge of every facet of it."

Actually, the mall is like a small city within a larger one to which it is in many ways beholden. The manager must have the O.K. of the Town Board, Planning Board, appeals board, fire department, and police department, as well as the cooperation of local politicians in order for the mall to operate.

---

*Most of the following material is based upon data attained from mall managers and tenants, during in-depth, taped interviews.

In short, the mall manager occupies what is in many ways a politically sensitive position in the mall hierarchy.

In addition to the mall manager and his staff, Shoptime has a board of directors. The board is comprised of the mall manager, the marketing director, the managers of the two major department stores, and nine other members voted into office by the members of the Merchant's Association. All mall tenants are obliged by contract to belong to the Merchant's Association and each pays monthly dues based upon the size of the store they lease. Among other things, the Association confers with the manager and marketing director on promotional campaigns and other undertakings designed to enhance mall businesses or public relations. According to some merchants, the "major's" typically control the Merchant's Association, and smaller businesses have very little to say about the running of the mall. Promotional efforts will be considered in greater detail in this and later chapters.

Presented below is a formal organizational chart of a typical shopping center. It includes developmental, operational and promotional aspects of mall life (Applebaum, 1970, p. 19).

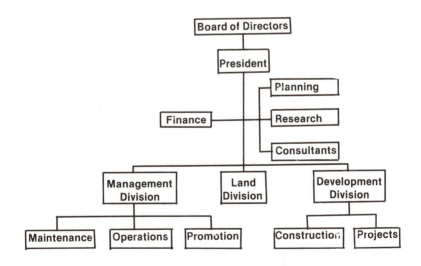

This is followed by a more limited organizational chart of the mall proper.

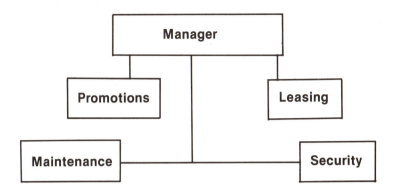

Tenant Leases

All tenants sign a standard mall lease that is modified and tailor made for each individual tenant. Seventy-five percent of all tenants at the Shoptime Mall are national chain stores. The tenant mix, with regard to percent of national chains versus independents, varies from mall to mall. For example, the mix of independents and chain store tenants on one large Mountain View California Mall is about 50-50.*

While the details of the tenant's lease vary, each covers certain basic "exhibits" or areas of legal obligation. The total Shoptime Mall lease is sixty pages long. The "main lease" occupies 20 pages. This is supplemented by different "exhibits." For example, there is an exhibit on the "site plan" displaying the entire shopping center. A second exhibit covers the actual configuration of the store. The third deals with what work the mall owners will undertake on behalf of the tenant prior to his arrival, and what work the tenant is responsible for in setting up his place of business. Another exhibit covers air conditioning expenses. Here the mall is allowed to increase the rates to the tenant as the local power company increases its rates to the mall. The next exhibit (about 30 pages long) is a detailed section dealing with construction plans and costs. These plans must be submitted to the mall by the would-be tenant in writing prior to their execution. In most cases, tenants are responsible for all construction costs associated with their business. Exceptions are made for the "majors" or "anchors" which are wooed with "tenant allowances." The final exhibit is electricity. The mall is responsible for providing electricity, air conditioning and maintenance, but the tenant pays a certain monthly fee to cover these services. As the rates to the mall increase so do the tenant's fees. Other mall expenses extend outside

*Information obtained from the mall's promotional director.

the mall proper and include such items as parking lot lighting and snow and trash removal. The above outlines what each member of the Merchant Association pays toward general mall maintenance, i.e., the "common area charge" but does not include additional expenses incurred for the actual running of any particular business, e.g., in-store security, advertising, employee costs, or maintenance.

Mall space is usually leased in one of the three ways outlined in Chapter 1. Because of the current popularity of malls, by far the most prevalent form of leasing is the "X" dollars per square foot, plus all of the costs outlined above associated with the "common area charge." The cost per square foot varies from mall to mall from as little as a few dollars to as much as $100 per square foot, per year (Trier, 1983).

There is, however, another factor that figures into this formula. In addition to this "base rent," that is, the minimum guaranteed rent cost of "X" dollars per square foot, it has been fashionable for some time now for owners to charge an additional fee that ranges from 2% to 10% of gross sales (current averages are about 6%) above the tenant's base rent. This practice is referred to as "overage." It is with this in mind that the mall manager has a person collecting and posting monthly gross sales figures. Under this system the better the individual store does, the better the mall owner does. This cost has been increasing steadily, and some tenants have begun to complain, usually to no avail. The exceptions again are the "preferred tenants." Since this cost often amounts to a good deal of money and there is no legal way to avoid paying it (it is included as a part of the standard lease) many tenants have taken to "underreporting" sales figures.

> In 1982, the findings (of one statistical study) show a staggering 66% underreporting of sales by all types and sizes of retailers examined. Unfortunately today there are more than 130 techniques utilized by retailers to misreport sales (Lamy, 1983).

Another authority indicates underreporting of 44% (Shopping Center World, January 1981). To cope with this source of potential loss, owners have (especially in the last 10 years) audited tenants to uncover "misunderstandings in the lease language" resulting in "underreporting" and losses to the owners. There is also another reason for the owners to want to catch instances of underreporting. The general standing of the mall is calculated in terms of the average sales per square foot of the center as a whole. "Underreporting" helps drive down this average and the mall's general "track record." In short, while "right to audit" clauses are usually a part of most mall leases they are not always systematically enforced.

Such is the general format of the lease at the Shoptime Mall. As for how long leases run, this varies with the tenant and the time that the lease was drawn. In the early days of the mall development leases for 25 years were not uncommon. Currently, leases generally do not exceed 5 and are sometimes for as little as one year. Short term leases, as well as all of the other expenses incurred by the tenants listed above, are clearly to the mall owner's advantage. The exceptions are the major department stores that the mall owners need in order to attract other tenants. These preferred tenants frequently build and own their own facilities and pay no rent at all. They also provide for their own security and advertising and are generally not subject to the disadvantaged leasing arrangements of smaller chain stores or independents.

We have considered above some of the ways in which tenant leasing agreements generally favor the owners. There are sometimes other advantages that accrue to mall owners not only over their tenants but over their would-be competitors as well. For example, a mall that was established earlier than others that sprang up in the same general locale may have written into its leasing agreement that stores opening on the first mall are not allowed to open on future malls located within a radius of "X" number of miles. This is a distinct advantage to the owners of the first mall in that "tenant mix" is crucial, and the first mall is by this agreement most likely to acquire the best choice of tenants. However, as we have noted earlier, the ideal "tenant mix" is not acquired by exacting laws of commerce but by trial and error. This sometimes allows for the success of newer malls at the expense of older established ones.

Shopping Mall Growth: Some Vital Statistics

As indicated at the beginning of Chapter 1, the expansion of shopping centers in the United States has been phenomenal. To get a more detailed understanding of this growth rate we will refer below to a survey conducted by the staff of *Shopping Center World* (Walker, 1981). The following statistics are from this source and cover the years 1979-1980.

While there were (as of the end of 1980) 268 shopping centers in the country with over a million square feet of gross leasable area (GLA) and several with over two million square feet, two-thirds of all the nation's shopping centers are of the "small" variety, that is between 10,000 and 100,000 square feet. These "small" malls account for 14,586 of the total 22,050 centers in the country and represent 30.8% of all shopping center sales. The small "strip size" malls also show by far the highest sales per square foot, $148.63, or $18 above the average for centers of all sizes.

At the time of the survey, California had by far the greatest number of centers (2,813) and South Dakota the fewest (34). A regional comparison shows the Plains states with the greatest percentage of gain in the number of new centers opened between 1979-80 (27.9%), an increase of 371 shopping

centers in a two year period. The far West follows with an increase of
21.8% or 655 centers, while the Northeast had the lowest growth rate, 9.6%
for an increase of 388 centers. It also had the lowest growth rate in terms of
sales figures, showing a 28.9% increase in the two year period. All other
regions of the country showed an increase of over 30%, with the Plains
states leading again with 46.1%.

As of January 1, 1981 there was an amazing 2,962,701,000 square feet of
GLA in all U.S. shopping centers of over 10,000 square feet. A more recent
survey (Shopping Center World, 1983) indicates an increase in total GLA
from 2,962,701,000 square feet in January 1981, to 3,238,918,000 square
feet in January 1982. A summary of this study indicating the economic and
physical growth of U.S. shopping centers is given below.

United States Total

January 1, 1983

	No. of Centers	Total GLA (Sq. Ft.)	1982 Sales ($)
10,000 - 100,000 sq. ft.	15,483	898,732,000	136,657,000,000
100,001 - 200,000 sq. ft.	4,622	706,221,000	93,579,000,000
200,001 - 400,000 sq. ft.	1,762	513,964,000	66,910,000,000
400,001 - 800,000 sq. ft.	886	521,400,000	67,639,000,000
800,001 - 1,000,000 sq. ft.	264	238,772,000	31,402,000,000
More than 1,000,000 sq. ft.	287	359,829,000	48,529,000,000
Total	23,304	3,238,918,000	444,716,000,000

January 1, 1981			% Gain 1982 vs. 1980		
No. of Centers	Total GLA (Sq. Ft.)	1980 Sales ($)	No. of Centers	Total GLA (Sq. Ft.)	Annual Sales
14,586	798,470,000	118,677,000,000	6.2	12.6	15.2
4,420	653,755,000	81,203,000,000	4.6	9.7	15.2
1,695	483,066,000	58,646,000,000	4.0	6.4	14.1
839	486,562,000	58,457,000,000	5.6	7.2	15.7
242	218,197,000	26,984,000,000	9.1	9.4	16.4
268	322,651,000	41,534,000,000	7.1	11.5	15.8
22,050	2,962,701,000	385,501,000,000	5.7	9.3	15.4

Categorical Analysis

	% of Total Centers	% of Total GLA	% of Total Sales	Average Size	Average Sales Per Sq. Ft. ($)
10,000 - 100,000 sq. ft.	66.5	27.7	30.7	58,046	152.06
100,001 - 200,000 sq. ft.	19.8	21.8	21.0	152,796	132.51
200,001 - 400,000 sq. ft.	7.6	15.9	15.1	291,694	130.18
400,001 - 800,000 sq. ft.	3.8	16.1	15.2	588,488	129.73
800,001 - 1,000,000 sq. ft.	1.1	7.4	7.1	904,439	131.52
More than 1,000,000 sq. ft.	1.2	11.1	10.9	1,253,760	134.87
Total	100.0	100.0	100.0	138,986	137.30

Shopping Center Industry Progress

	No. of Centers	Total GLA (Sq. Ft.)	Gross Sales ($)	Average Size (Sq. Ft.)
1982	23,304	3,238,918,000	444,716,000,000	138,986
1980	22,050	2,962,701,000	385,501,000,000	134,363
1978	19,201	2,498,303,000	283,050,000,000	130,113
1976	17,458	2,277,930,000	211,504,000,000	130,480
1974	15,074	1,874,259,000	153,087,000,000	124,337
1972	13,174	1,649,972,000	123,159,000,000	125,245
1964*	7,600	1,010,000,000	78,700,000,000	132,985

*Based on a survey conducted by SCW's Editorial Consultant, S.O. Kaylin.

Current Trends

Recently, there has been a trend among shopping mall developers that runs in two directions. First, is a tendency to build smaller malls, and secondly, a greater effort is being made to redevelop urban centered malls.

There are a number of reasons for the developers interest in "downsizing" and urbanizing mall development, many of which explain both trends at once. First is the availability of large parcels of suburban land appropriate for mall development. It is now easier to find two smaller parcels than one large one. Secondly, the development of smaller centers is less expensive than large ones, not only to the owners, but to the tenants. The increased density of stores in small malls reduces the cost per square foot by dividing the development costs over a broader base, i.e., building a greater number of smaller stores in a given area. Thirdly, the developer benefits by building a number of small centers in a given geographic area (versus one large one) by allowing the developers to "test the market at different levels" and (not incidentally) to simultaneously "wipe out your competition" (Opsata, 1980). Finally, as the traffic in metropolitan areas increases, it takes longer on the average to get to any single location. Scattering smaller malls gives the potential consumer easier access.

All of this says nothing of the point noted earlier, that smaller malls have the highest sales per square foot and are consequently most profitable, not only to build but to operate.

There are other economic considerations for downsizing malls. This trend which began with the 1980's promises (according to some spokesmen) to continue (Opsata, 1980).

> Ten or twenty years ago, construction costs were about one-third of what they are now, real estate taxes were about one-third of what they are now, energy costs were probably one-tenth of what they are now, and the minimum wage and hospitalization benefits and selling costs were all a fraction of what they are now. All of these have increased at a far greater rate than productivity per square foot. So we are still tightening up.''

While these and other economic considerations have to do with the trend toward developing smaller malls, they are also responsible for a move to revitalize urban centers. There is a certain irony here. Given that the development of suburban malls was in large part responsible for the decay of urban centers in the first place, why all this interest on the part of developers to revitalize downtown areas? The interest in this case, as in all cases with mall development, turns on the profit motive. The expanded interest in urban redevelopment promises to produce greater profits than the developer's exclusive efforts at continued suburban mall expansion. Not only is suburban property with good demographics becoming increasingly scarce and expensive, but potential urban based mall property has become correspondingly cheaper. Municipal authorities give attractive tax breaks and other economic incentives to developers, which have made the redevelopment of urban centers (around malls) more attractive. There has also been increased social pressures to revitalize urban centers. In many cases these have even been supported by suburbanites in search of ''culture'' and a more cosmopolitan environment than suburban malls offer.

The trend of revitalizing urban centers characterizes the thinking not only of American developers but Canadians as well. One author on this topic puts it this way (Weiss, 1980):

> In fact, downtown redevelopment (in Canada) is the new focus of activity, after ten years of chasing (and capturing) the suburban dream, many developers are back where retailing action began. Whether in small towns of large, they're finding the pickings profitable, the opportunities surprisingly plentiful (in the inner-city).

These Canadian redevelopment projects, such as the Eaton Centre in Toronto, Edmonton Centre in Edmonton or the Scotia Square in Halifax, were frequently of the "mixed-use" variety. That is, they offer a mix of office space and retail tenants. This, as you may remember from Chapter 1, characterized some of the early malls in the United States and is currently a feature of many new urban redevelopment projects in this country.

Major projects of these kinds are planned long in advance and new regional and larger centers often require from five to ten years to materialize. There are many expenses associated with this time lag. For example, legal expenses alone for a relatively small 350,000 square foot Canadian center cost the Ontario Municipal Board a quarter of a million dollars (Weiss, 1980).

As is true in this country, the growth rate of shopping centers in Canada has slowed. The boom period of the 1970's that found every major Canadian city ringed with regional malls is a thing of the past. One Canadian shopping center group manager put it this way (Weiss, 1980).

> We can put the damn thing up faster than the population can grow.

The U.S. experience has been similar. There is a slowdown on the expansion of new centers. Those being built are generally smaller, and there has been expanded interest on the part of developers in urban redevelopment of the "mixed-use" variety.

Most efforts in the U.S. have been undertaken through the renovation of existing inner-city buildings (Opsata, 1980). One representative of the firm of Taubman Company (estimated by many to be the largest developer of leasable retail space in North America) notes:

> Our Market Analysis suggests that there are upwards of one hundred communities around the country that are candidates for significant retail development as part of downtown revitalization strategy.

Taubman Company had (as of 1980) 50% of its active projects located in downtown areas (Opsata, 1980).

In addition to the reasons given above for the trend towards urban redevelopment (centered around retail and office use) there are other incentives for would-be developers. Apart from the growing scarcity of good suburban parcels of land, the flight to suburbia has slackened between 1950 and 1970, and most metropolitan areas have shown increased growth as the result of this reversal in urban to suburban migration patterns. The rising cost of energy has also made many people increasingly reluctant to drive to suburban malls.

Furthermore there has been a shift in the general public desire to revitalize urban centers. Those in the immediate area are interested in revitalization because they are obliged to live in the "urban blight" the suburban dream helped create. Those in suburbia are interested because they increasingly bear the bulk of the tax burden for the inner city which has traditionally been the heart of culture and cosmopolitan atmosphere for the suburbanite. Inasmuch as suburbanites pay for these services, (in large part) they have, at least in recent years, become more interested in their efficiency and accessibility.

The federal government has also been instrumental in the developing interest in urban redevelopment. In 1980 a significant amount of money in the form of Urban Development Action Grants (UDAG) was targeted to help the inner cities. In addition, the Carter administration funneled money into the central cities for mall development by allowing city officials to request the cut-off of federal funds to support services that had a negative impact on urban retail areas (Opsata, 1980). This was rather like the Canadian government's efforts to put constraints upon the expansion of suburban and urban based malls that flourished at the expense of existing small retail businesses.

While there is considerable disagreement as to whether more money can be made in suburban or urban centers, there is another split in thinking among those who opt for urban redevelopment investment opportunities. First, there are those that feel that "downtown" must ultimately compete with suburban based shopping centers and can only successfully do so by having traditional "anchors" that offer a range of merchandise not otherwise available at suburban malls. In contrast to this view are the iconoclasts who maintain that there are many economically successful "anchorless" downtown developments. These draw potential customers not by traditional "anchors," but by hotels, offices, the nearby natural environment or other untraditional sources of population draw (Opsata, 1980).

The Economic Impact of the Mall

We have thus far considered in various contexts the reciprocal effect of the mall on the community and the community on mall life. The economic impact of the mall has been discussed only peripherally. Let's now take a more detailed look at Oldtown area malls (the site of this study) as a special case, and then go on to some more general observations of the economic consequences of mall expansion.

Local Effects

The Old town area has several shopping malls. The discussion that follows will deal with only three of them. The combined resources of these three facilities contribute in a significant way to the economic wellbeing of the entire community. For example, the Shoptime Mall, built in 1975, has

115 stores, an enclosed area of 750,000 square feet, and parking for in excess of 4,000 cars. The Candyville Mall has 52 stores, covers 607,796 square feet, and has outside parking for 3,251 cars. The Fairgrounds Mall which was first opened in 1959 (and enclosed in the 1960's), contains 66 stores that employ between 8 and 900 people. It has parking for 2,287 automobiles, a GLA of 465,000 square feet and a total enclosed mall area of 545,000 square feet. For a schematic diagram of the Fairgrounds Mall depicting the number, kind and location of tenants, see Figure 3. A "tenant mix" list for the Candyville Mall is given in Table 1. A map of the Shoptime Mall giving this information will be presented later in Chapter 4.

Combining some of these statistics for these three malls, we see that they provide combined parking facilities for about 10,000 cars, employ about 3,000 people, and offer a combined retail sales area of about one and three-quarter million square feet of space. This says nothing of the employment the actual construction of these facilities created.

The statistics of the average number of shoppers per day given by the manager of the Fairgrounds Mall was about 10,000. Given that Fairgrounds has about three-fourths of the area and about one-half the stores that Shoptime has, a fair estimate for Shoptime might be 15,000 customers per day (a more realistic figure than that quoted by the Shoptime Mall manager in the next chapter) and about 8 or 9,000 per day for the Candyville Mall. Combining these statistics, there is in the neighborhood of 35,000 customers a day that frequent these three facilities and much more during holidays and the Christmas season. With these figures in mind, we have only to add the customer traffic generated by the three or four other major malls in the same general geographical area to see that a substantial percent of all shoppers in the Oldtown Statistical Metropolitan area (SMA) are mall shoppers.

This is consistent with the national statistic noted earlier in Chapter 1, that 50% of all retail sales in the country are shopping center sales.

While the mall generates jobs for the local community, they are nearly all low-paying jobs. As we will see later, employees of the mall are nearly all part-time employees and poorly paid. Because of their part-time status, their fringe benefits are nearly nil. Wages for mall employees start at $3.50 - $4.00 per hour. They are given 20 - 40 percent pay increases "at regular time intervals." The national minimum wage at the time of the study was $3.35 per hour. Employees at one of the malls studied averaged about seven years of service.

Tenant employees fair about as well. Many are paid minimum wage upon entering the job. One part-time employee who has worked in one of the "majors" at the Shoptime Mall for about two years as a saleslady in jewelry and costmetics (and has a college degree) now makes $3.70 per hour.

Figure 3
Fairgrounds Mall 1979-80

1. Sears
2. Dey Brothers
3. The Gap
4. Wells & Coverly
5. Kinney Shoes
6. Spencer Gifts
7. Flah's
8. Baker Shoes
9. David's
10. Fabric Tree
11. G.C. Murphy Co.
12. Paper Poppy
13. Lori B
14. Addis Co
15. Lerner
16. Foxmoor
17. Gerber Music
18. Ceo & Rutz Shoes
19.
20. Huckleberry Finn
21. Onondaga Savings Bank
22. Fotomat
23. Casual Corner
24. Denby's
25. Charney's
26. Stylish Women
27. Midtown Shoe Repair
28. The Pet Gallery
29. Patricians Bakery
30.
31.
32. Red Cross Shoes
33. VIP
34. Baskin Robbins
35.
36. Dr. Gramsey
37. Fairway Restaurant
38. Thom McAn
39. Kay Jewelers
40. Coleman Florist
41. Zizza's Hairstyling
42. Joe Charles Sports
43. Sneaks 'n Cleats
44. VIP Yarns
45. Terra Art
46. Tuxedo Junction
47. Wilson Jewelers
48. Fanny Farmer
49. Walden Book
50.
51.
52. Orange Julius
53. Yackety Shack
54. Manufacturers Hanover
55. Marine Midland
56. Hickory Farms
57. Irene Shop
58. St. Clair Paint & Wallpaper
59. First Savings
60. Pavone's
61. Chess King
62. Radio Shack
63. Tobacco Village
64. Tops & Bottoms
65. Toy & Hobby
66. Friendly Ice Cream

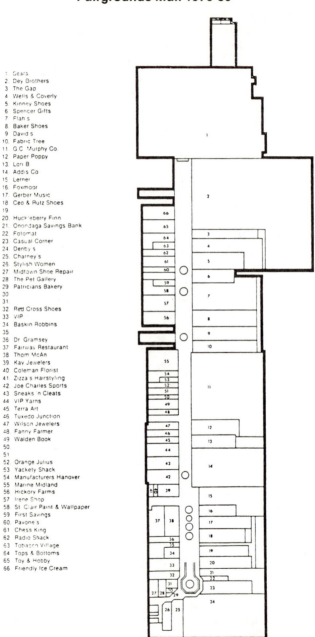

Table 3
List of Stores and Shops in the Candyville Mall

1. Fashion Island	27. Liberty Travel
2. Blank (unoccupied store)	28. Greenhome
3. Sweets by LDJ	29. U.S. Postal Service
4. Blank	30. Anderson-Little
5. Creative Pantry	31. Pizza Time
6. Blank	32. Altier's Children's Shoes
7. B. Dalton Books	33. General Nutrition Center
8. Winslow Sporting Goods	34. Christina's
9. 16 Plus (under construction)	35. Blank
10. Old West	36. Gallenkamp Shoes
11. Recordtown	37. Blank
12. Regis Hairstylists	38. Hanover Shoes
13. The Earring Tree	39. Blank
14. JoAnn's Nut House	40. Pretzel Shop
15. Blank	41. Blank
16. Aladdin's Castle	42. Bill Gray's Restaurant
17. The General Store for Pets	43. Blank
18. Reed's Jewelers	44. Shoes to Boot
19. Canaltown Country Store	45. Blank
20. Blank	46. Butler's Shoes
21. Kinney Shoes	47. Blank
22. Fashion Bug	48. CVS Drugs
23. Blank	49. Jo-Ann Fabrics
24. Blank	50. Scott's Hallmark Shop
25. Command Performance	51. Dew Sterling Optical
26. Carhart Camera Center	52. K-Mart

Another part-timer on the same mall who works as a cook in the mall's largest restaurant earns $3.65 per hour. He is a graduating high school senior. Teenagers working in the fast food establishments as salespersons all receive similar pay and next to nothing in fringe benefits.

Consumers

We have listed elsewhere a series of expenses that the tenants must absorb. For example, in the case of a small jewelry store on a "going mall," rent may be 25 to $30,000 per year and insurance (which has become for jewelry stores the second most expensive item) another 20-$25,000 a year. The jeweler must be insured for employee bonding, fire, hold-up, burglary, products the consumer is hurt by or claims to be hurt by, workman's compensation, coverage during the transfer of jewelry outside the boundaries of the store proper, and so on.

In addition, the jeweler must pay all expenses associated with the building and opening of his store, the short lease, the stocking of the store, employee costs, advertising, in-store security, "overage" and Merchant Association dues. In short, opening a modest jewelry store on the mall represents a considerable cash outlay, and a substantial "nut" (overhead) on a routine basis. Someone must absorb these costs, and that someone is ultimately the consumer. If mall shoppers like shopping malls, they should. They are, in the final analysis, paying for it. Of necessity, things cost more on the mall than they used to in free standing stores with much lower overhead and initial establishment costs. Many, especially working and lower class customers, recognize this additional cost, and use the mall for a comfortable, convenient, safe place to "kill time" or entertain themselves, but shop elsewhere.

Developers and Owners

If the consumer pays more, those working at the mall are paid low wages, and small tenants are at a distinct disadvantage vis-a-vis the "majors" and developers, how do the mall owners do in the mall business? As a matter of fact, developers have done extremely well. A typical 100,000 square foot center can bring the owner a profit of 60-70 percent of the cash investment upon its sale. One trade journal, *Shopping Center Guide,* sees shopping centers as "money machines" (Lorimer, 1978).

Developer's profits come from basically two sources, rents and the sale of centers. We have discussed earlier the various ways in which leases are drawn to insure the developer profits from rents. Sales of centers are also very lucrative. Among other things, income from the sale of centers is generally taxed as capital gains, which is less than half of the tax rate of ordinary income (Feagin, 1982). Profits are insured to the developer in other ways as well. Lending agents such as banks, insurance companies or foreign investors have also made huge profits from shopping center financing. They in turn insure attractive profits to developers by giving them preferential treatment in the borrowing of money. As developers give "majors" and "chains" preferential treatment, lenders give developers financial benefits contingent upon many of the same factors. For example, by way of securing their loans, lending agents prefer developers to rent to national chains. Those who do so get preferential treatment. It is no accident that close to 75% of all mall tenants are national chains and that this is true even when renting to independents would be more lucrative for the developer.

Because the development of malls is not as lucrative or certain a venture now as it was in the 1970's, many lending institutions have recently sought to further secure their loans by requiring developers to cut the lending agent in on the actual ownership and profits of the mall. "Tight money" has of late, frequently obliged developers to comply with these new lending and borrowing practices for large scale developments.

Foreign Investments

The loaning of money for shopping center developments is not only a popular investment in this country, but abroad as well. Overseas investors at the year end of 1979 had direct investments of 52.3 billion dollars in all U.S. industries. This represents "the net book value (at that time) of foreign direct investors' equity in, and outstanding loans to, their U.S. affiliates" (Opsata, 1981). Of this total, 1.7 billion dollars of foreign money was invested in U.S. real estate. While substantial, this figure badly underestimates the total asset value of U.S. real estate owned by foreign "parents." The reasons for this are as follows:

> It (the 1.7 billion dollar figure) includes only direct investment in U.S. affiliates that are classified in the real estate industry. Direct investments in affiliates in other industries, which may hold real estate, is classified in the industries of those affiliates. Furthermore, the portion in real estate affiliates reflects only the portion of total real estate held by such affiliates that is financed with funds from foreign parents. That portion may be small relative to the total because real estate investments usually are highly leveraged — the ratio of loans (largely from unaffiliated sources) to investors' funds used for equity purchases normally is high (reprinted in part from an August 1980 publication of the U.S. Department of Commerce, Bureau of Economic Analysis).

Not only is foreign investment in U.S. real estate considerable, but a sizeable segment of it is in shopping centers. Shopping centers are generally considered more secure investments than office buildings (Opsata, 1981).

> Seventy to 80% of the cash flow is generated by major tenants with national credit ratings...When they looked at office buildings they might see only 5% or 10% of the tenants with national ratings and others...that just come and go every three to five years.

Notwithstanding the greater security in shopping centers, foreign investors have increasingly been turning to office buildings (Opsata, 1981).

> The profit ability of a center is based on the concept of percentage rents (''overage''), and there's a general perception now that spendable income is decreasing. Less sales means less percentage rents.

For investors who continue to be interested in shopping centers, the interest seems to be in the larger regional malls. The majority of overseas investors are institutions from the Netherlands and Great Britain. While pension funds constitute the largest portion of this market, insurance companies are substantial investors as well. Institutions not only represent the largest segment of investors, but threaten to take the entire market. The typical minor institutional investment is between 3 and 5 million dollars. Major investments are on the order of 100 million dollars (Opsata, 1981).

Government Subsidies

We have noted earlier, the federal government's role in the expansion of shopping malls as a part of urban redevelopment through the issuance of Urban Development Action Grants. The preferential tax treatment that the government extends to the developer is another case in point. These official-unoffical government subsidies extend into the realm of local government as well. Indeed, the very existence of shopping malls is contingent upon local governments providing the infrastructure for mall life. We have in mind here such essential services as sewage, gas and electric, zoning and rezoning of land, utilities and road building, most of which are financed through municipal bonds and funds. In real terms, these represent a governmental subsidy for mall developers in the form of development capital.

While the developer must solicit and acquire the cooperation of local government, and the latter becomes in this sense a kind of partner, the developers do what they can to retain control over essential mall decisions, e.g. its location, architectural design, parking facilities, traffic problems, noise and/or other pollution problems, and questions of urban or suburban planning in general. All of this has a give-and-take aspect. The municipal government not only gives the would-be developers legal access to mall land and essential services, but gets in return increased employment and taxes (not only from the developer and tenants but from the increased value of surrounding properties as well). However, even in the area of reciprocal benefits, the mall owners usually benefit most.

Promotional Efforts

While there is still a wide range of opinion among mall tenants as to which is the shortest road to the bank, most believe that you need to promote business to succeed in business. Mall promotions represent mall expenditures. As previously indicated, these expenses are born by the tenants through the Merchant's Association. Who contributes and how much to these promotional campaigns has led some mall promotional directors to speak of "good and bad" tenants.

While some tenants actively contribute to promoting the mall, others are viewed as "parasites" that feed off the traffic that the "good" tenants generate. Some leases allow for merchants to pay only merchant association dues, but not necessarily any additional advertising or promotional costs. Other leases require all merchants to pay both and eliminate the problem of "parasites."

Indeed, not all parasitic merchants hope to succeed in business. Some independent businesses are started in hope of showing a loss. As one promotional agent at a large California mall put it:

> Doctors set their wives up in the gift business (or something) on the mall. They don't do anything to participate in mall promotions. They are parasites. The losses they incur actually serve as a "tax shelter" to doctors who write off losses and actually come out ahead. This is of course good for them but bad for the mall.

For those who hope to succeed in business by increasing customer traffic there are generally two basic approaches. One is to benefit indirectly by increasing traffic on the mall proper through promotional campaign contributions designed to benefit the mall in general. The other is a more personal direct benefit approach designed to get potential customers not so much to the mall, as to one's place of business. The latter has little faith in the "trickle down" theory of economic gain. Allowing that all Merchant Association members contribute monthly dues to the maintenance, security and promotion of the common area segment of the mall, the "majors" usually undertake their own promotional campaigns and rely little if at all on the "trickling down theory" of success. Smaller tenants of course benefit indirectly from these independent efforts of the "majors." The following are some examples of the kind of campaigns that the mall and its tenants offer in attempting to increase their patronage.

We will find toward the end of Chapter 5, a long list of possible public shows, exhibits, and involvements designed to draw customers to the mall. Recent innovations allow for the expansion of that lengthy list with such items as concerts, jogging and bike paths around mall property, trout fishing on the mall, public bus stations on private mall property, and performing ballet companies (Sullivan, 1981).

Maximum efforts are made for "grand openings" and the Christmas season trade. For example, the grand opening of Ingram Park Mall in San Antonio, Texas, drew a host of celebrities who were chosen to appeal to all social, economic, gender and age strata (Citron, 1981).

> Vic Tayback (Mel of "Alice" fame) was chosen for his blue-collar appeal. Jim Ryan, Olympic running champion, was brought in to the opening because statistics show that the average jogger is white collar with an average yearly income of $35,000. Ed McMahan, Simon's (the promotional agency's) "Master of Ceremonies," appeals to women ages 35 to 55...Lou Brock appeals to sports fans (he holds the record for most consecutively stolen bases), Clayton Moore (The Lone Ranger) for his family appeal...and so on.

The promotion campaign described above was hooked into a fund raising effort for the "Special Olympics" and other grand opening events that continued at the San Antonio Mall for a month. These activities were of sufficient local interest to involve the media. In fact, promotional directors always seek to encourage the participation of the media. Such involvement offers the mall free radio, T.V. and/or newspaper coverage and to a wider constituency than is otherwise possible with limited mall funds. In short, good promotional directors try to produce an "event," something that is newsworthy and in the "human interest" vein.

Not all promotion efforts are on the grand scale described above. Like they say, "Texans think big." Another San Antonio mall located on the West Coast has a total annual promotional budget of only $65,000. Sixty thousand of this comes from "Merchant Dues and Landlord Contributions," and $5,000 from "Directory, Table rentals (from shows) and other." The promotional efforts of this mall are outlined below in the form of an in-house memo.

Approved 1983 Promotional Budget
(Based on Current Dues)

Estimated Income:

Merchant Dues & Landlord Contribution	$60,000
(Landlord's Contribution was $20,000)	
Other Income (Directory, Table Rentals, other)	5,000
Total Estimated income Based on '82 Dues........................	$65,000

*This data was acquired from a taped interview with the promotional director.

Estimated Expenses:

Advertising & Promotional Expenses

Paid Advertising

Newspaer (space & production)	$20,000
Radio (time & production)	9,800
Yellow Pages Advertising	1,400
County Map Guide	650
Discover Magazine	1,550

Promotional Costs

Graphics, Signs, Flyers, Printing, etc.	$ 600
Promotional Events	3,000
Total Advertising & Promotional Costs	$37,000

Operating Expenses

Promotion Director Fee	$24,000
Telephone Service	1,800
Petty Cash (sign changing, misc.)	1,500
Professional Fees (legal, other)	700
Total Operating Costs	$28,000

Additional Landlord Contributions

Bookkeeping & Secretarial Services
Christmas Decoration Storage & Installation
Office Space

Total Estimated Expenses................................... $65,000

February Bulletin

President's Weekend Promotion

Advertising for the **Presidents' Sale** weekend will run on Wednesday in the *Alto Weekly* and *Alto Town Crier/Mountain Sun.* The ads will feature the *Diet Coke Taste Giveaway* promotion with additional radio advertising backup on KGA. Diet Coke will be sampled on the mall Friday, noon to 8 p.m.; Saturday, 10 a.m. to 6 p.m. and Sunday, noon to 5 p.m. Coupons for a '83 Ford Thunderbird giveaway will be distributed at the Coke tables and deposited at the display car on the mall. Store tie-in material is available for the asking.

Pre-Spring Promotion March 26-27

An **"Outdoor Living & Garden Fair"** will be conducted on the mall Saturday and Sunday, March 26, 27. It will feature gardening and other outdoor activities in a series of lecture-demonstrations by prominent gardeners and organizations.

Fashion shows are also scheduled and participating stores are invited to contact the new manager of Clothestime (948-5211) for details.

March Meeting, Friday the 4th

Regular monthly Board of Director meetings will be held in the Association Office above H&S Florist at 8:30 a.m. on the first Friday of each month. All members in good standing are invited to attend.

Mall Directory Update

Revisions (many of them) of the three mall directories will be ordered within the next week or two. Please let Mr. B. know quickly if you plan any name changes or have any corrections from the existing directory. Please understand that it will take a few months for these to be completed.

'83 Promotions/Lists Attached

We hope you find the 1983 Promotion Schedule, Calendar and new store/phone list helpful during the coming year. It will be a year of growth through cooperation.

Mr. B.
Promotional Director
948-8004/327-1469
2/14/83

1983 Proposed Promotion Schedule

Thursday-Monday February 17-21	Presidents Day Sale Event
Wednesday-Sunday March 23-April 3	Outdoor Living — Gardens & Cooking with Fashion Shows if desired
Thursday-Sunday April 21-24	**Sidewalk Sale
Thursday-Sunday April 28-May 1	Mountain & Whish School Districts Annual Student Art Show
Saturday-Sunday May 14-15	Alpha Pi Used Book Sale
Friday-Sunday June 17-19	Spring Travel Show & Fashion Shows if desired with KLA & Suntrips of California

Sundays July 3-August 21	Sunday Summer Concert Series, Series of eight co-sponsored with MPTF of AFM
Thursday-Wednesday August 18-24 (7 days)	**Annual "Gold Rush" Back-to-School Event and Sale
Saturday & Sunday September 24-25	Open Theme Community Event
Thursday-Sunday October 13-16	**Sidewalk Sale
Saturday, November 19	Holiday Preview Night in Hollywood Theme in cooperation with AMC Theatres (Sat. Night Openings)
Friday-Sunday November 25-27	Santa Arrival Weekend
Friday-Sunday December 2-4	**Early December Christmas Event & Tabloid
	**Major Retail Sale Events

presented 12/3/82
revised 1/12/83

Since the part-time free lance promotional director's fee was $24,000 per year, this left only $40,000 annually for a regional size mall. With this in mind, the small number of events catalogued above is in no way surprising. Merchants at this mall relied primarily upon "Sidewalk Sales."

To give the reader a better idea of the promotional efforts of management and tenants on shopping malls of different sizes, the following statistical summary is offered. This data on the prevalence and relative contribution of merchant associations, promotional funds and management, was extracted from a trade publication (*Dollars and Cents of Shopping Centers: 1981*).

To begin with, the percent of shopping centers with merchants' associations depends primarily upon their size. You will remember in chapter one, shopping malls were defined as "small" (25,000 to 400,000 square feet of GLA), "intermediate" (400,000 to 600,000 square feet of GLA), or "large" (600,000 or more square feet of GLA). However, in the trade, shopping malls are defined by the Urban Land Institute as follows: "neighborhood centers" (typical size 50,000 square feet of GLA); "community centers" (typical size, 150,000 square feet of GLA); "regional centers" (typical size of 400,000 square feet of GLA), and "super regional centers" (typical size 750,000 square feet of GLA). This latter categorization scheme will apply to the statistics that follow.

Ninety-eight percent of *super regional,* 95% of *regional,* 58% of *community* and 22% of *neighborhood* centers have merchants associations. Only 1% of *super regional,* 3% of *regional,* 4% of *community* and 3% of *neighborhood centers* rely on a promotional fund. Finally, 1% of *super regional,* 38% of *community* and 75% of *neighborhood centers,* have no form of association for promotional purposes. Almost all centers (about 95%) that have merchants associations or promotional fund assessments, base them upon the extent of the tenants use of GLA.

However, this last statistic is somewhat deceiving. You will remember from our earlier discussions how in shopping malls (as well as out of them) "the poor pay more." That is, the "anchors" typically receive preferential leasing terms and pay less per square foot for rent and everything else. This is also true of promotional costs via merchant association assessments. *Super regional* centers report a median total amount raised for merchant association activities of 17 cents per square foot of GLA. Department stores in *super regional* malls typically occupy the greatest percent of the mall's total GLA, yet they contribute only 4 out of every 17 cents of merchant association money collected for promotional purposes. The center's management contributes 3 cents and all other tenants 10 cents. The situation is similar for *regional* size centers. Here the median total amount raised by the merchants association is 16 cents per square foot of GLA. The department stores contribute 4 cents, management 4 cents, and all other tenants 8 cents. The receipts raised by *community* sized shopping centers is only 10 cents per square foot of GLA, but here too the non-anchor tenants pay the lion's share. Finally, the median total receipts for promotional purposes for *neighborhood shopping* centers is 13 cents per square foot of GLA.

In summary, whether promotional efforts are run by the merchants association as in larger malls, or a promotional fund as in some smaller malls, the "anchors" and management pay less and the other tenants pay more. In fact, the statistical breakdown is as follows:

In super regional shopping centers	**Median % of total raised**
1. Amount raised from department stores	23%
2. Amount raised from other tenants	50%
3. Contribution by center management	21%
4. Other sources	11%

In regional shopping centers	**Median % of total raised**
1. Amount raised from department stores	21%
2. Amount raised from other tenants	49%
3. Contribution by center management	24%
4. Other sources	13%

Community shopping centers	**Median % of total raised**

1. Amount raised from junior	16%
   department stores
2. Amount raised from other tenants	64%
3. Contribution by center management	22%
4. Other sources	7%

Neighborhood shopping centers	**Median % of total raised**

1. Amount raised from tenants	76%
2. Contribution by center management	22%
3. Other sources	25%

With slight variations, these figures are representative of Canadian shopping centers as well.

Summary

We have presented in this chapter some of the local and national economic implications of mall life. In a variety of ways we have dealt with the economic effects of malls on downtowns, small businesses, urban redevelopment, suburban growth, mall tenants, mall employees, mall developers, and the public at large. It has been accentuated throughout that "mall business is all business," and that the profit motive is first and foremost in the minds of the developers, tenants and consenting municipalities. While the unlimited acquisition of money as an end in itself was early recognized as a central feature of capitalism (Weber, 1948), the crassness of this undertaking in the case of shopping center developments, has perhaps reached a new high water mark.

Extremes in all areas, frequently prompt extreme statements and often from unlikely quarters. For example, General Douglas MacArthur, perhaps the most belligerent U.S. general in recent history, is reputed to have said in connection with the awesome destructive power of the atomic bomb, "War is outmoded." Victor Gruen, a famous architect and one of the early pioneers of shopping mall development in this country, upon seeing the way in which shopping centers were developing from the 1950's to the 1970's, said, (shortly before his death in 1980) that the original idea of the suburban center had been perverted by "fast buck promoters and speculators" (Shopping Center World, April 1980). Gruen's disenchantment should come as no surprise. His early mall designs (the Northland Shopping Center in the 1950's) called for pedestrian malls filled with sculpture gardens, landscaping, and public auditoriums, all to be in easy reach and integrated into existing established social spaces. Of course, innovative planning of this sort did not necessarily allow for the acquisition of cheap land, standardization, maximum profit per square foot or easy maintenance. A a result, the success of Gruen's early mall designs were abandoned. Later developers were not attempting to build a better social world. Their vision was much less grandiose and much more plebian. They sought only to maximize the returns on their investments. This led to the kinds of malls to be described in this work, and not the grand design that Gruen and some other early architects had envisioned. The extend of this abandonment is best illustrated with a quote from the promotional director at one mall whose job it was to encourage business:

> "God, have you spent any time at indoor shopping
> centers. I used to manage one. They're depressing."

References

Applebaum, William. 1970, *Shopping Center Strategy.* International Council of Shopping Centers.

"Audits Just Part of Mall Routine." 1981, *Shopping Center World,* January, p. 120.

Citron, Rusty. 1981, "Booking Right Celebrities Means Knowing Center's Market." *Shopping Center World,* April, pp. 42-46.

Feagin, Joe. 1982, *Building Capitalist Cities.* New Jersey: Prentice Hall.

Lamy, Kenneth S. 1983, "Landlords Losing Money by Neglecting the Right to Examine Tenant's Sales." *Shopping Center World,* February, p. 68.

Lorimer, James. 1978, *The Developers.* Toronto: James Lorimer and Co.

Opsata, Margaret. 1983, "Good Things Come in Small Packages." *Shopping Center World,* April 1980, pp. 28-32.

Opsata, Margaret. 1981, "Retail Properties Slip to Second Place as Foreign Investors Pursue Offices." *Shopping Center World,* February, pp. 27-30.

"People and Places." 1980. *Shopping Center World,* April, p. 10.

"Statistics for 1980-82 Show Big Shift to Expansion GLA." 1983, *Shopping Center World,* January, pp. 21-36.

Sullivan, William. 1981, "State/Province Reviews." *Shopping Center World, February, pp. 40-46.*

Trier, Beth. 1983, *San Francisco Chronicle.* Thursday, February 3, p. 19.

Walker, Gail Brown. 1981, "Center Industry has Grown to Major Proportions." *Shopping Center World,* January, pp. 65-80.

Weber, Max. 1948, *The Protestant Ethic and the Spirit of Capitalism.* (Trans. by T. Parsons, with forward by R.H. Tawney) London: Allen and Urwin.

Weiss, Gary. 1980, "Canadians Set Sights on Small, Large Downtowns." *Shopping Center World,* December, pp. 20-25.

Chapter Four

The Shoptime Mall: A Case Study

Built in 1975, the Oldtown Shoptime Mall covers an area of 100 acres. The enclosed portion encompasses some 750,000 square feet, while the outdoor segment has parking for 4,000 automobiles. Prior to that, from 1959 till 1975, there was only a strip of uninviting and unenclosed stores, most of which were demolished to make way for the new facility.

The mall is basically a one story, L-shaped building which includes a basement floor in two of the large department stores, as well as in other smaller portions of the mall proper. The "service area" of the mall, e.g., the shoe repair, tailoring, hair stylist and watch repair, are located at the far end of the mall in one of these lower levels. The entire facility is kept at 75° in the summer and 68° in the winter. Shoptime and two other local malls are owned and operated by Eagan Associates.

According to the mall manager, the number of shoppers frequenting the mall varies by the day of the week, time of day and time of year. In general there are more shoppers on weekends (estimates for Saturday range from 22,000-100,000 per day) than on weekdays (6,000-30,000).* Most daytime customers are women. Some are older persons but most are young adults and middle aged. Teenage girls are also much in evidence, primarily on weekends and during the school vacations. In fact, the manager estimates that 70% of all shoppers are women. The large number of stores catering to women reflects this statistic. More men shop during the evening than during the day (and more on weekends than weekdays). Apart from restaurant goers, very few of either sex frequent the mall from 4:30 to 6:30 p.m. or during the dinner hour. According to the manager, Christmas sales represent roughly 25% of total annual sales for some businesses and as much as 75% for others.** This is probably an underestimation in that it

*The author believes these estimates to be wishful thinking on the manager's part. After all, there are only about 250,000 people in the Oldtown Metropolitan Area. That nearly 50% of these people should find their way to Shoptime on any one day is very unlikely. Indeed, the Sherman Oaks Galleria (Mall) now immortalized in the song "Valley Girl" only draws 11 to 15,000 persons on a Saturday (Capaldi, 1982).

**The above data was obtained for the most part from an hour-long tape recorded, transcribed interview with the mall manager and is supplemented in places by material from my field notes.

has been noted elsewhere that approximately half of all national sales occur in the last three months of the year.

Nearly all the mall's stores (117 in all) line both sides of the long L-shaped corridors. The low ceilings contribute to the customer's experiencing a kind of tunnel effect. Seventy-five percent of all tenants are national chain stores. The kinds of stores and their locations are given in the Shoptime directory and map found below and on subsequent pages.

Shoptime Mall

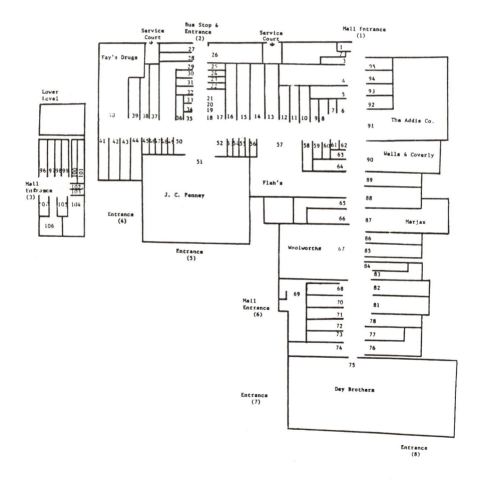

Shoptime Mall

Women's Apparel

The Addis Company 91
Barbara Moss 14
Casual Ms. 42
E. Cramer 88
Flahs 57
Foxmoor Casuals 71
Fuleihan's 27
The Half-Size Shop 74
Lerner Shops 4
Lori B 15
Tops 'n Bottoms 73
Ups-n-Downs 85

Men's Apparel

Charney's Mens &
   Boy's Stores 29
Chess King 70
Dougles Stone Ltd. 43
Flahs 47
Mr. Shop 16
Proving Ground 68
Togs 'n Bootery 28
Tops 'n Bottoms 73
Wells & Coverly 90

Children's Apparel

The Addis Company 91
Altier's Stride Rite
   Bootery 50
Charney's Mens &
   Boy's Stores 29
Small World 64
Wells & Coverly 90

Financial Services

First Savings 1
Manufacturer's Hanover
   Trust Company 63
Savings Bank 55

Specialty Apparel

Down Under Leather 24
Life Uniform 48
Mr. Tops 45
Parklane Hosiery 9

Sheba's 94
Tuxedo Junction 47

Shoes

Altier's Stride Rite
   Bootery 50
Connie Shoes 10
Kinney Shoes 86
McKay Shoes 65
Naturalizer Shop
   Shop 84
Regal Shoes 62
Sheba's 94
Sneaks n' Cleats 105
Thom McAn 66
Wells & Coverly
   Florsheim Shoes 90

Jewelry & Gifts

Carousel Gifts 82
C.J. Buller Ltd. 95
The Gift Horse 37
H.J. Howe Inc. 89
Kay Jewelers 52
Richard & Co. 58
Treasure Hut 59
Wilsons Jewelers 92

Entertainment/Sports/
Leisure

Base Camp 23
Gerber Music 83
Great Games 100
Liberty Travel 96
Marjax 1st Place in
   Sports 87
Radio Shack 38
Sneaks n' Cleats 105

Restaurants/Fast Foods

The Baron's 35
Bergsons 77
Eric & Ralph's 5
The Magic Pan
   Restaurant 2
Orange Julius 54

Pavone's Pizza 11
T.J.'s Big Boy Jr. 81
Cork Steak House 26

Specialty Stores

A&E Wigs 46
The Bedroom 104
C.J. Buller Ltd. 95
Coleman Florists 93
Color Copy Center 22
Down Under Leather 24
Elhoff Gallery 7
Fotomat 33
Fraden Lock 21
Harvey's Watch &
   Jewelry 103
Mr. Tops 45
Old Erie Coffee
   House 60
Peddler's Pouch 17
The Pet Department 30
The Phone Booth 19
Phone Center Store 36
Plants Plus 18
Shoe Service &
   Leather Haven 97
Singer Company 41
Small World 64
So-Fro Fabrics 76
The Tinder Box 53
VIP Yarns 39

Books

Coles The Book
   People 13
Economy Book &
   Stationary Story 44

Personal Services

A&E Wigs 46
Barber & Styling
   Center 98
CVS 78
Community Library 79
Harvey's Watch &
   Jewelry 103

Joseph Anthony & Co.	99	Sindoni Custom Tailoring	102	Nature's Pantry	31
Dr. John P. Kavanagh, Optometrist	107	WI-TV	61	Old Erie Coffee House	60
Kelly Lyn Figure Spa	3	**Specialty Foods**		Sweet Temptation	49
Merle Norman Cosmetics	25	Baskin-Robbins Ice Cream	8	Tiffany's Bakery	12
New York State Job Service	69	Bavarian Pretzels	34	**Variety/Drugs**	
Shoptime Management Office	80	The Bread Basket	20	Fay's Drugs	40
Shoe Service & Leather Haven	97	Carmel Corner	32	F.W. Woolworth Co.	67
		Fanny Farmer Candies	9	**Department Stores**	
		Hickory Farms of Ohio	72	Dey Brothers	75
				J.C. Penney	51

Outside the Mall

Viewed from the parking lot the Shoptime Mall appears in the form of two large brown brick rectangles intersecting each other at right angles and located on an even larger rectangular parcel of land. In a generous view, the building can be described as functional. One edge of the L (the long side) is adjacent to a major municipal thoroughfare while the other sides of the building are surrounded by paved parking lots. These are divided into some semblance of sanity by a combination of roadways, stop signs and island dividers. From a distance, the grassy dividers appear as specks of green on a macadam background. In the evening the entire area is lit by powerful sodium floodlights atop high aluminum poles. This produces a kind of eerie aura outside the mall.

Finding a parking spot is rarely a problem, even on a busy day. One has access to the parking lot from two city streets with three entrance and exit points, and the entire complex is located about three blocks from a freeway exit that is a major east-west artery. All of the above is contiguous to a better section of suburban Oldtown, but not so far removed from the city proper as not to draw on customers from other parts of town as well. This is done with the assistance of the municipal bus service as well as special buses for students and older persons. In short, from the outside, one could say that the mall has a functional look, is demographically well situated and provides easy access and adequate parking.

From the parking lot, the names and general location of the major mall establishments are clearly marked by signs along the top of the outer edge of the building.

Inside the Mall

While most customers reflect very little upon the unesthetic exterior of shopping malls, they do tend to describe "good" and "bad" malls (at least in part) in terms of their interior design. This is perhaps not surprising when we realize that, apart from the initial approach to the shopping mall and parking one's car, one spends all of one's time inside not outside the mall. It is inside that one conducts one's business, shops, socializes or otherwise seeks entertainment. This is not to say that potential customers are totally unconcerned about the outside appearance of the mall or that a mall with a reputation for crowded or unsafe parking lots will not suffer a loss of business. However, if it is true as Goffman (1959) and others suggest, that it is the "presentation of self" (the presentation of the *outer* person) that counts in describing and understanding social interactions in everyday life, it is the *inner structure* of the mall that is most important for describing and explaining the social life of malls. Mall customers almost always refer to what's going on inside (not outside the mall) when telling of their satisfaction or dissatisfaction with mall life. With this in mind, it would be reasonable to suppose that mall builders and owners would pay great attention to the interior design of shopping malls. The fact is that they rarely do.

While a wide range of architectural designs are found in mall interiors, and some are much more esthetically pleasing than others (these are more often found in avant-garde "upper class" malls) malls generally are larger extensions of the national business chains they house. That is to say, one has the distinct feeling that if you've seen one, you've seen them all, and they are not very esthetically pleasing. Why should this be? As noted in Chapter 1, this standardization is undertaken in order to minimize capital investments, and maximize net profits for the builder and owners.

In a T.V. "C.B.S. Reports," dealing with the Oak Park Mall in Kansas (1982), Charles Kuralt asks the question... "Why did the nearby Country Club Plaza Mall, one of the first built in the country in the 1920s and still considered to be architecturally superior to the Oak Park Mall, (and others like it), not become the model for future malls?" The answer? Developers found that you could spend less money, build inferior settings and people would come anyway so long as they were *safe, warm,* and *dry.*

I think this is true. I doubt that the success or failure of shopping malls is primarily owing to their architectural design. While a factor in the equation (like being well situated, having easy access, or providing adequate parking) there are other reasons why some malls succeed while others, that look essentially the same, fail. The bottom line, I feel depends more upon how successful the mall managers are in attracting "the right mix" of businesses and otherwise organizing things so as to promote and encourage an agreeable and stable social life for mall customers.

At least some mall managers are aware of this need. The manager of the Oak Park Mall spells this out when he tells his T.V. interviewer that he wants the customers to feel at home and be comfortable on the mall. The longer they stay and the more they come back, the better the mall does. In an effort to insure that customers stay long and return often, the manager trys to organize things so that the mall is not just a convenient place to shop, but offers one a "free" source of entertainment... "We want them (the customers) to consider the mall a part of their entertainment."

Safety and comfort (the other key features of mall social life) are not neglected either. Oak Park is kept at 68^0 in winter and 72^0 in summer. Safety on the mall is not a serious problem. One guard put it this way:"I've got to look out for the interests of the mall. What we got here mostly is a lot of kids, a few shoplifters. It's nothing compared to what's out in the city — nothing like that." This is of course true. One encounters very little overt crime or disturbance on the mall. As indicated in Chapter 1, social life on the mall is characterized by "nothing unusual is happening." The orchestrated management of mall life that allows for the customer feeling that they are enveloped in a protective environment is achieved at a price. The Oak Park Mall Manager put it this way:

> Some people think malls are too controlled — take the 'verve' out of life
> at a shopping center which is possibly so. But its nice to know that
> your wife and kids can come out to Oak Park Mall and not run across
> a wino out back there by the compactor.

All of the above characterize the efforts of the Shoptime manager as well. Given that all malls try (some more successfully than others) to encourage and promote an acceptable social life for their customers, by providing for their *safety, comfort and convenience,* and *entertainment,* how do mall owners, builders and managers go about it, and why do some succeed while others fail?

"Feeling Safe": A Product of Inside Security

The feeling of safety one experiences on the mall is a direct product of security measures the mall evokes. To begin with, the mall is not what it most often seems to be — a public place. The rules governing appropriate mall behavior are not the same as those found in public places. Since malls are private property, one is subject to the rules of the mall builder and operator in addition to civil laws applying to public places. For example, the U.S. Supreme Court has ruled that one may not distribute antiwar leaflets upon a privately owned shopping mall the way one is free to do in the public domain (N.Y. Times, July 9, 1972). Even the Salvation Army's Christmas fund raising efforts have been banned (Pollock, 1982). Another case in point was a colleague of mine who asked some of his undergraduate students in a course on sociological methods to conduct a survey on the mall. The four had hardly begun this project when they were asked by mall security if they had acquired permission from the mall manager. When they said no, they were unceremoniously asked to leave.

One author on the topic put it this way (Carpenter, 1978):

> Security has somewhat different surface meanings to owner, tenant, and shoppers, but basically these individuals are bound by a common interest. They do not want the normal operation of the center disturbed or interrupted by unfriendly forces. To the owner, security connoted the preservation of the buildings representing his investment and maintenance of peace and order, the absence of which will deter shoppers. To the tenant, security revolves around protection of his merchandise and employees, plus that same interest in a peaceful environment for his customers. In the mind of the shopper, security has to do with personal safety and the safety of property while in the center or traveling to and from it.

Uniformed or Plain-Clothes Security

Many (perhaps most) shopping malls have uniformed security guards. Generally speaking the existence of full-time security forces seems to follow about the same pattern of incidence as full-time managers. Both are rare in centers of 400,000 square feet (or less) and usual in centers of 600,000 square feet or more. Very large centers employing 30 or more security people have what amounts to a private police force (Carpenter, 1978).

Security forces are frequently dressed like police officers or state troopers and probably to good effect. Uniformed security personnel are hired by the mall manager and their services are usually paid for by mall tenants as part of their leasing package. This proviso is covered in a section of the lease dealing with "common area" expenses. Uniformed guards sometimes carry guns, usually night sticks, and often walkie-talkies in order to communicate with other guards, custodial personnel and the mall manager at the central control center. Many, but not all, uniformed security guards are older retired men (sometimes former police officers). They are usually poorly paid and trained and because of their part-time status their on-the-job fringe benefits are negligible.

Some indication of the minimal training that shopping mall security persons receive can be had from the account of a one-time security guard who was hired at a large local mall eight years ago (about 1974), upon its grand opening.

> I sent a resume to a post office box (to apply for the job of security guard) but got no reply. Four months later I saw another ad, went to the mall for an interview with Gene Management Security Company, and

was given the job at $2.75 per hour. I was fitted for a uniform, trained
for 2 or 3 days, worked for two weeks and was fired.''

When asked why he was fired, my informant gave the following account. In
it the reader can easily see why he lasted only two weeks. He had breached
the most basic rule of all mall life by disrupting decorum.

Some guy drove through the parking lot fast, so I chased him and
caught him. I cussed him out (for being inconsiderate and creating a
hazard) and the customer cussed back and reported me to the manager
and threatened to sue. I was fired.''

Here we have not only a breach of decorum, but an incident that threatened
community relations and a lawsuit. All of this insured my informant's early
retirement from a life as a security guard.

In regard to hiring "moonlighting" police officers, the trade book noted
earlier (a guide for Mall Managers) offers the following advice:

One approach to the security problem sometimes successfully used is the
employment of off-duty policemen from the community...such
personnel can be quite effective at relatively low cost...however, there
are sometimes latent political problems that can surface without warning and create unfavorable publicity...at one time, the managers of
small centers often handled their security problems by an off-the-record
arrangement calling for a little something under the table to the local
police chief, or precinct captain, but that practice also has waned as law
enforcement has become increasingly political.'' (Carpenter, 1978)

The above seems to recommend in a roundabout way that bribing local
police chiefs to get their cooperation in hiring moonlighting off-duty police
officers is (or was) one way to get an inexpensive trained security force for
some (usually smaller) mall settings.

While most malls have uniformed guards, a minority of others use only
plain-clothes persons. This is true not only for the security people who
patrol the mall proper, but for the separate security forces within the larger
department stores. In general, store security may be uniformed and obvious
(as a deterrent to theft or disruptive behavior) or incorporate unobtrusive
plain-clothes officers, who seek not to deter crime, but to catch criminals or
social transgressors.

Armed or Unarmed Security

Apart from the pros and cons of hiring uniformed versus plain-clothes
security people, there is the question of whether or not to arm them. Proponents of the unarmed-guard approach feel that it enables them to hire
relatively low-skilled persons on a part-time basis whose major duties

consist in directing traffic, controlling disorderly children and generally monitoring mall activities. If "real trouble" erupts unarmed guards are encouraged to call the local police or fire department for backup help. Proponents of the higher paid, better trained armed guards, argue that some people (depending upon the area that the mall is located in) have no respect for authority unless guards are armed. Indeed, in some metropolitan areas it is virtually impossible to employ unarmed personnel.

An interesting aside on the apparent shortage of trained armed security guards is a recent article in the *New York Times* (October 31, 1982) that reports:

> Jobs for librarians were declining, but those for security guards were rising. As a result, the new report said last February, Montgomery County Community College in Blue Bell, PA. was "replacing a library science program" with "a weapons training program that the college says will be the first of its kind in the country.

"In House" or "Farmed Out" Security

There are also advantages and disadvantages to hiring your own security force. Those who employ their own forces usually employ a full-time head of security. This person runs the security team within the store and acts as a kind of manager in charge of hiring and firing store-based security personnel. In other cases department stores do not carry their own full-time security on the payroll but "farm" that function out to professionl agencies that are responsible for hiring, firing, bonding, paying and ensuring the presence of security forces to guard the store on a day-to-day basis. Some large stores prefer this arrangement because it frees them of this responsibility entirely and in some contractual arrangements frees the store owners (with the inclusion of a "hold blameless clause") from the possibility of being sued for false arrest or the mistreatment of customers.

The owner of one New York City security firm interviewed by the author, who provides uniformed guards to a large woman's wear chain located in shopping mall settings, described the arrangement in this way. The store owners pay him $7.00 per hour to place a uniformed guard in each of two stores. He pays the guard $4.00 to $4.25 per hour. Two guards working different hours for a total of 72 hours a week cover one store. This costs the store owners about $500 per week, per store or a security cost for two mall stores of about $4,000 per month. While a considerable outlay, the owners feel that the peace of mind, reduced "shrinkage," and general sense of well-being that customers experience in the presence of uniformed guards, make the enterprise worthwhile. This security head also confirmed what was noted earlier, i.e., most loss through theft occurs not by way of shoplifting customers, but store employees. One example of such in-house loss was noted on a recent local T.V. newscast (8-21-82) which reported a $6,000 theft by the stockroom supervisor of the J.C. Penney Store on the Shoptime Mall. However, a video tape showing the stolen articles leads the author to think that the "shrinkage" was greater than reported.

Another benefit to store owners of subcontracting security is that the store owners don't have to pay for employee benefits, e.g., workmens' compensation, overtime costs, vacation time, retirement funds or health insurance benefits. The sum total of these, represent a considerable cash outlay that is absorbed by the $4,000 per month paid in the above example.

In Store Security

Approaches to in-store (as opposed to "common area," i.e., on-the-mall) security practices can be had by considering Dey Brothers, one of the two large "anchors" on the Shoptime Mall. This store has its own security force, and instead of obvious uniformed guards, takes the unobtrusive plain clothes approach. Members of its "security teams" are supposed to look like average shoppers. Their "teams" know and converse with the uniformed mall police and the security officers and teams in the other stores on the mall. Members of one store's security team may follow customers into another team's territory and enlist the second team's aid in arresting the shoplifter or troublemaker. They do not, however, (according to one employee's account of the store's security routines) attempt to arrest a shoplifter within another security team's territory. This practice of recognizing and respecting territoriality in the security business was corroborated by the accounts of a one-time uniformed security guard noted earlier.

The greatest "shrinkage" in Dey Brothers occurred in the women's section, in the junior's and sportswear departments. Costume jewelry, where items were displayed on the counter within easy reach, also experienced considerable loss. Customers at Dey Brothers who are caught shoplifting may, or may not, be prosecuted, (the many signs to the contrary notwithstanding) depending on what they "lifted" and their reaction upon being caught. If they are not caught stealing large amounts of merchandise, are not known as repeated offenders, and are cooperative and contrite, the store usually refrains from pressing charges. This is rather like the probation officers approach to wrongdoing by juveniles. Those who get off with lighter sentences are those who admit their sins, are cooperative and contrite, and promise not to repeat the errors of their former ways (Cicourel, 1968). This account of Dey Brother's security policy with regard to petit larceny was in direct contradiction to the mall manager's statement. According to him, all tenants have agreed in writing to prosecute shoplifters so that the mall can minimize embarrassment and the possibility of suits for false arrest. Another strategy large stores sometimes invoke to help insure against false arrest, is the use of time-lapse or constant T.V. recording systems that cost about $6,000. "Security guards feel more secure about arresting people if the deed is on film." (Seely, 1982)

Sales personnel at Dey Brothers who witness a customer shoplifting may not approach or directly confront the shoplifter. Procedure in such a situation dictates that the salesperson call the "cash officer" or operator, report the theft, and ask for an intervention on the part of the security team. Apart from shoplifting and disturbances, security is also called upon to check out discrepancies in incoming merchandise or cash register receipts.

The head of the security team in this store is a woman, who has three men under her direct command. While a fair sized department store of this kind may have four or more in-house security persons, smaller stores on the mall rely exclusively on salespersons to monitor customer activities, and report thefts. Whether or not approaches and/or arrests are made, every effort is made to keep the matter as "obscure as possible." In short, the watchword here as in all mall business is decorum. In this regard, mall security is rather like police work outside. Officers are frequently less interested in enforcing the law than in keeping the peace (Bittner, 1967).

"Common area" Security

Having discussed some general features of mall security and some specific examples of how they apply to Shoptime stores, let us now consider "the common area" security forces at the Shoptime Mall. Shoptime employs its own common area security forces, that is, those persons paid to guard the corridors of the mall proper. The entire force is comprised of one full-time head of security and 15 part-time guards. Additional security is added during busy holiday seasons on an as-needed basis. According to the mall manager, security personnel earn between $5.50 and $6.00 per hour, much more than one would expect in light of the earlier quote that guards elsewhere usually receive much less. The reason for all the part-time security help (as well as part-time store employees in general) is the financial gains that accrue to the mall. Part-time help receive no fringe benefits.

While the Shoptime mall manager indicated that statistics were compiled on mall crimes and breaches of the peace, he was unwilling to share these figures with the author. He did venture a rough estimate of one person per week being apprehended for shoplifting. As indicated earlier, a recent change in the general mall lease at Shoptime requires all tenants to prosecute shoplifters. This requirement is not uniformly enforced. There are many reasons for this. First is the possibility that a tenant who prosecutes offenders may be sued for false arrest. Secondly, bringing charges for petit larceny requires a lot of effort and time on the part of the store owner and manager. Thirdly, convictions against shoplifters are hard to come by. The mall manager put it this way:

> I mean, the problem these days is that the courts are very sticky about the fact that you have to catch the person red handed. You can't assume anything. So a lot of people are very hesitant about calling our office because they are worried about lawsuits.

Finally, it is not clear that convictions when they are forthcoming are a deterrent either to the one convicted or others. This makes the monitoring and enforcement of customer theft a difficult, expensive, time consuming, and frequently frustrating business. However, the extent of store theft (from within and without) warrants the effort. "Shrinkage" contributes to annual national losses of billions of dollars. Employee theft is estimated by one source to be six times that of customer theft (Seely, 1982).

The Mall and Crime Statistics

In order to get some independent assessment of the extent and kinds of mall crimes, the author compiled a list of charges reported by the local police. These are noted on a regular basis in the Thursday edition of the local paper along with all crimes committed in Oldtown and surrounding areas. This effort yielded the following results.

Nearly all crimes committed at shopping malls are crimes against property as opposed to crimes against persons. Heading the list is petit larceny (shoplifting). When petit larceny charges are brought against an adult their name, address, offense, and the merchandise allegedly stolen are given. The following is illustrative:

> Petit larceny charged: Helen H., 44, of Kings Gates Apartments, was charged with petit larceny August 5. She is charged with taking clothes valued at $44.15 from Sears store at Fairgrounds (a local mall). She was to appear in court at a later date.

Most, but not all offenses are of this variety. Some are more serious.

> Pair Arrested: Albert J., 24, of 181 South State Street, Oldtown, and Warren D., 20, of 131 South State Street, Oldtown were charged October 4, with third-degree burglary and third-degree criminal trespass at Spendville Mall. Both were taken to the Public Safety Building jail in lieu of $5,000 bail apiece.

Crimes against juveniles for any offense leave the juvenile's name and address unknown. This anonymity is guaranteed to juvenile offenders by law.

> A 19 year old Oldtown woman was charged with petit larceny August 5, in the village. The woman's name was not released as she may be eligible for youthful offender status. She was charged with taking two locking gas caps valued at $22 without paying for them. She posted $50 bail for reappearance in court Wednesday.

However, for some reason, recent entries have sometimes listed the juvenile's name.

On very rare occasions one finds a reference to crimes against persons either on the enclosed part of the mall proper, or in free standing buildings that are sometimes a part of the greater mall property. The following is an example of the latter:

> Assault alleged: Kevin and Brian S., 20 year old twin brothers, both of 60 Walnut Street, Oldtown, were charged with second-degree assault August 5, in connection with an incident at Poor Richard's Pub in the Candyville Mall. They allegedly punched and kicked Jeffry Foster. They were committed to the Public Safety Building for reappearance in court at a later date.

Even rarer are potentially dangerous offenses against persons on the mall proper. The following appeared as a separate article and not a part of the usual police reports.

> A 17 year old boy was charged Tuesday with first-degree attempted robbery after he allegedly drew a hunting knife on an arcade manager in the Marketplace Mall.... He was arraigned before the Town Justice, and released on $500 bail.

The following is a breakdown of shopping mall related crimes in the area as reported in the *Oldtown Standard* for a 5 month period, beginning with May 1, through September 30, 1982.

Combined Total Number and Kind of Offenses on Oldtown Area Malls from May 1 — September 30, 1982

1. Petit Larceny	**36 Cases**	
	"Youthful Offender Status"	17 cases (13M, 4F)
	Adults	19 cases (8 M, 11F)
2. Grand Larceny	**1 Case**	
	Adult	1 case (M)
3. Possession of Stolen Property	**5 Cases**	
	Juvenile Offender	5 cases (F)
4. Possession of Marijuana	**5 Cases**	
	Adults	3cases (1M, 2F)
	Youthful Offenders	2 cases (sex not recorded)

5. "Bad Check"	**1 Case**	
	Adult	1 case (F)
6. Third Degree Burglary	**1 Case**	
	Youthful Offender	1 case (F)
7. Fourth Degree Criminal Mischief	**3 Cases**	
	Youthful Offenders	3 cases (M)
8. Obstructing Government Administration	**1 Case**	
	Youthful Offender	1 case (F)
9. Criminal Impersonation	**1 Case**	
	Youthful Offender	1 case (F)
10. Disorderly Conduct	**3 Cases**	
	Adult	3 cases (F)
11. Harrassment	**1 Case**	
	Adult	1 case (F)
12. Fourth Degree Possession of controlled substance (morphine)	**1 Case** Adult	1 case (F)

Total = 59

May 1 — September 30, 1982

Spendville Mall

Sears	4 cases
Carls Drugs	1 case
Herman's Sporting Goods	1 case
Price Chopper Market	1 case
Total Number of Offenses	7

Shoptime Mall

J.C. Penney's	13 cases
Dey Brothers Dept. Store	3 cases
Total Number of Offenses	16

Candyville Mall

Record Town	5 cases
Poor Richards Pub	3 cases
P & C Market	2 cases
Total Number of Offenses	10

Fairgrounds Mall

Addis Company	1 case
Dey Brothers	1 case
Total Number of Offenses	2

Merry Mall

Common Area	2 cases (Possession of Marijuana)
Behind Mall	3 cases (fourth degree criminal mischief)
Total Number of Offenses	5

County Mall

Price Chopper	2 cases
Radio Shack	1 case
Total Number of Offenses	3

Total = 43*

*The difference between the two totals, those on this page (43) and those found on the preceding page (59) results from the fact that this page lists the number of persons charged with offenses while the preceding page gives the number and kind of offenses. Some offenders were charged with more than one offense.

An analysis of the data reveals that there were 12 different kinds of offenses listed against all persons charged with illegal acts within major shopping malls in the Oldtown area from May 1, 1982—September 30, 1982. By far the greatest number of offenses fell within the category of Petit-Larceny (Shoplifting). There were a total of 36 cases of Petit Larceny noted in the local paper during this period. In a tie for the second place was "possession of stolen property" (5 cases), and "possession of marijuana" (5 cases). Third in rank (also a tie) was "4th degree criminal mischief" (3 cases) and "disorderly conduct" (3 cases). All other offenses listed only one case each within the above time interval. Disregarding adult or youthful offender status, there were a total of 59 offenses, 26 male, 31 female and two persons whose sex was not given.

Nearly all mall offenses (75%) occur in major anchor department stores or other large chain stores. The remainder occurred within the mall's common area, or on property outside of the mall. By far the largest number of offenses occurred at the Shoptime Mall. This is to be expected since it has by far greatest number of customers. In terms of reported crimes, it seems that there were *no* instances of crime among small mall tenants. Since this is extremely unlikely, one of four alternative explanations present themselves. 1) Mall security officers never catch shoplifters or other offenders in the smaller shops on the mall, 2) the owners of these establishments do not prosecute offenders who are apprehended, 3) offenders in these settings are apprehended and prosecuted but go unreported in police reports, or 4) such offenses are reported by police but are not considered newsworthy by reporters who do not include them in their weekly "police reports." While uncertain which of the above apply, the author is inclined to believe that the second alternative is most likely. As indicated earlier, prosecuting offenders is a time consuming and frustrating undertaking that frequently creates more problems for the mall tenant than it solves.

Some indication of the futility of trying to bring charges of petit larceny against adolescents can be had from the following verbatim accounts (Ksander, *et al.*, 1983).

Adolescent:

She took me out there, it used to be something else, but it's "Look-and-See" now. She stole un, a red and white terry-cloth, um short set for me. And she stole some white socks. She stole a lot of those terry-cloths, she stole one for me, for her. (Hmm) And, you know, for some other people too. And um, and we went, we, um, when she heard about some white sneakers in "Overshoes" and she wanted to get some. So uh, so we went to "Overshoes" and this lady kept following her in "Overshoes." You know, and she, she really wanted these sneakers bad. And so after, you know, the lady kept following her and, you know, she got upset, she says, "what you following me for," like that, right? And the lady said, "well I'm just doing my job," you know, she rolled her eyes an everything. (Hmm) And so, she didn't get a chance to get the sneakers and stuff. She was just walking around the store like she was going to buy something, you know. (Um humm) And so the lady kept following her, so she went all the way in the back of the store, and got a garden tool about this big and, and was walking back up in front with it. And, she start, she start walking real fast, and the lady thought she lost her and the lady ran right in front of her and she hit the lady with the thing. And um the lady fell down the stairs in "Overshoes." And um, she was just cussing at her and stuff. Then she left.
Q: They didn't press charges or anything about it?
A: No they just said don't come back in the store again.

Another adolescent had this to say:

I was going around and I walked into this record store and these, these things that come like this, the eyes that go across, you know? When I, it went beep, you know, when I walked through the things [the theft detector] and some guy started chasing me and stuff, and they caught me. Brought me to the police station. But they didn't say nothing, they just said uh, stay out of trouble, they didn't press any charges.

It should also be noted that it is unlikely that in the five month period reported upon above, six mall settings had only apprehended 36 shoplifters. After all, this would mean that over a 20 week period there was an average of 1.8 cases of petit-larceny per week in all six malls combined. Given that many thousands of people per day go through the Shoptime Mall alone (see figures noted earlier in this chapter) and the manager at the Shoptime Mall acknowledged about one person per week was charged with crimes, the above statistic seems very unlikely. It seems a better bet that large chain stores are also guilty of only token efforts at prosecuting cases of petit larceny, their written lease commitments to the contrary notwithstanding. In conclusion, it should be noted that mall crimes tend not to be serious and are almost always against property.

Inside Security and Outside Backups

We have discussed security within the mall — both in the stores and common areas. However, with respect to mall security strategy, "when the going gets tough, the tough don't get going" — they call for outside help.

> A centers' security force is an extension of and not a replacement for — public agencies. All managers must keep this fact in mind. . . . The night patrolman who believes a burglar is on the premises sends for the city police and lets *them* win any medals for ferreting out the trespasser. If it appears that a gang of professional car thiefs is working the parking lot, a ring of shoplifters is operating in the stores, put the matter in the hands of the local police detectives and let them set the trap (Carpenter, 1978).

This reliance upon local police to help maintain mall security is seen within the wider area of maintaining good community relations. Outside police are called upon to help in-house mall security with respect to five different areas of potential trouble, i.e., 1) pickets in labor disputes, 2) social demonstrations, 3) political candidates, 4) charitable solicitors, and 5) "obstreperous juveniles." Maintaining good community relations by maintaining mall decorum, is an essential part of mall security. Every effort is made to insure good public relationships with the greater outside community by presenting an external presentation of self that reflects a "nothing unusual is happening" stance. In this pursuit, congenial relations between the mall manager, internal security, and the outside local police force, is essential.

Having covered how a feeling of safety is produced for mall customers, let's go on to consider the question of comfort and convenience, the second major factor in any equation of mall social life.

Comfort and Convenience in the Common Area

The efforts of the developers, owners, and managers to provide for the potential customers' comfort and convenience on the mall takes many forms. First and foremost in importance is the mall's ability to offer a comfortable controlled indoor temperature. The thermostat at the Shoptime Mall is kept at a constant 75° in the summer and 68° in winter. In a climate where summers are characterized by high temperatures and humidity and winters by very low outside temperatures and prodigious amounts of snow, the mall offers one of the few hospitable environments available outside of the home. When we add to these conditions, a large suburban population of mall customers and their children who have lost the knack of hibernating or visiting with others in their homes during the winter season, and who get "cabin fever" after spending even a couple of hours at home, we can see how the mall has become for many "the only game in town." The fact that malls provide a large indoor controlled environment is per se a guaranteed draw, for such persons. In this sense malls (assuming that they are well situated) do not compete in any significant way with other institutions for customers. It is becoming increasingly true that the only other serious source of competition is other malls that may also be strategically located and do a better job of providing for the user's safety, comfort, and entertainment.

Apart from providing one with a comfortable indoor temperature and shelter from the outside environment how else do shopping malls provide for customer comfort? Actually there are many ways. For example, malls offer comfortable seating and rest areas within the mall's common area. Older persons can walk and rest at their leisure, younger persons can sit and "watch the action," while mothers and young children can get some respite at these way-stations during shopping sprees, or just sit awhile and "kill time."

In addition to common area seating, merchants frequently provide a "sidewalk cafe" atmosphere by placing chairs and tables with umbrellas within the mall corridors to encourage shoppers to buy food and drinks, and consume them within an artistic (indoor) "outdoor" setting. Here we have the notion of street corner society again, within the confines of the mall proper. These "sidewalk cafes" are frequent meeting places for teenagers, or groups of older persons, and provide a comfortable place to congregate and socialize.

Another attempt to produce a comfortable environment has to do with floor coverings. Shopping malls take two basically different approaches to floor coverage, i.e., the hard and soft approach. The hard approach refers not necessarily to the visual effect so much as the density of the floor covering material. As indicated earlier, every effort is made to minimize maintenance and maximize profits. With this in mind hard floor coverings are usually made of fired earthen tiles, vinyl tiles, or in the case of elegant upper-class malls, marble slabs or terrazzo floors made of polished marble chips imbedded in cement. While most malls need all the light they can get (many rely solely on artificial lighting) hard floor tiles are more often than not of a dark color, usually brown or rust. While this goes far to disguise dirt and wear, it does little to brighten the corridors inside the mall. The white marble used in some upper-class malls proves the exception.

Quite apart from the overall visual effect, many mall customers complain that hard floors are hard on the feet and make mall walking less enjoyable and comfortable than walking on soft floors. The latter are almost always short pile, easily maintained, long wearing, wall to wall carpet. Here again, dark hued carpeting is almost always chosen in the name of easy maintenance. While reasonable on this score, such colors help produce an easily recognized, otherwise undesirable long, dark corridor look. To help moderate this effect, dark rugs are sometimes borken up by patches of light colored tile strategically located in front of fast food establishments. This helps reduce the drab effect, serves to enhance the lighting and helps provide for easy maintenance. Keeping the Shoptime Mall clean is an outside contractor who employs a staff of seven custodians. Two additional "in-house" custodians clean and care for the rugs. An "in-house" maintenance superintendent services 110 HCV's (heating, air conditioning and ventilation units) and two others are employed to care for the outside area. These efforts are not wasted. Everything always looks well maintained.

Other Conveniences

Other sources of comfort and/or convenience are the numerous mall establishments themselves. As noted earlier, malls contain (among other tenants) post offices, employment agencies, food markets, coffee shops, banks, fast food establishments, barbershops, beauty salons, and travel agents. All of these provide in a variety of ways for a wide range of centrally located consumer conveniences. This is true not only from the perspective of providing convenient shopping and necessary everyday services, but more generally by offering convenient, comfortable public settings for meeting and socializing. Coffee shops, department stores, beauty salons, and restaurants are some examples of places used for these purposes. The routine use of such facilities as social gathering places among the elderly in retirement settings has been noted in the earlier works of the author (Jacobs, 1974, 1975).

One source of comfort and convenience conspicuously absent in many mall settings is restroom facilities sometimes referred to as "comfort stations." The frequent absence of restrooms in the mall proper is a mystery to the author. Some of the settings reported upon in this study (the Shoptime Mall is a case in point) have no restroom facilities within the common area of the mall. For a facility that deals with thousands of people a day, many of whom remain for hours, such an omission would seem a serious oversight.

The objection can be raised that some restaurants and large department stores have restroom facilities and that customers can always use those in an emergency. The fact is restaurants discourage the use of their restrooms by anyone other than their own customers, and often say so with strategically placed signs. The restrooms that are available in department stores are always discreetly located and difficult if not impossible to find.

The question arises, why all the reluctance to provide convenient restrooms, or to make alternative tenant facilities public knowledge? Actually, there are several reasons. One is that restrooms occupy space that could otherwise be rented for 15 to 20 dollars per square foot. Secondly, they involve an additional initial outlay of capital by the builder and developer, an outlay that offers no potential dollar return. These are the sorts of investments that developers studiously seek to avoid. Thirdly, restrooms require maintenance and maintenance costs money. Finally and perhaps most importantly, public restroom provide a potential setting for crime against persons (the sort of crime malls especially seek to avoid), as well as other sorts of offenses such as "tea room trades" (casual homosexual activities in public restrooms). The author inadvertently blundered in on a situation of this sort in the restroom of an upper-class department store that anchored one end of a large shopping mall in Northern California.

Notwithstanding the initial expense of building and maintaining restrooms and the potential for offensive public activities that they may harbor, not to provide such facilities breaches one of the malls major rules of thumb, i.e., providing for the customer's comfort and convenience. This is an especially serious problem for older persons. This oversight has been largely remedied in many of the newest malls which include not only restrooms, but "community rooms" for public services.

Another customer convenience provided by the mall is not so much concerned with producing contentment on the mall, as insuring that people can get there in the first place. While most suburbanites drive (and outside convenience is well covered by easy access and parking) other customers ride the buses. Apart from the developers arrangements with local government to provide bus service to the mall, the mall owners and/or tenants sometimes pay for the subsidized busing of certain targeted populations, such as students and older people.

The manager of the Shoptime Mall described one such experimental pilot program in this way:

Manager: ...what we're doing right now is we're busing elderly people in from seven different homes on the eastside of town on Thursdays. Every Thursday from 10 in the morning until 3 in the afternoon we have a bus running, a Centro (city) bus running...we started (this service) in September (1982) and the last week of the scheduled run will be next Thursday (October 21, 1982)...and we set it up on a trial basis to see if it would be in our best interest as well as everyone's benefit; and it was to run for four weeks...we were hoping the number would be in the hundreds (because that is what the payment for the bus would require to make it economically feasible).

Interviewer: How has it been working so far?

Manager: The first two weeks were not successful; we had 25 people one day (Thursday) and 22 the next week...they were very disappointed about the lack of attendance and have sent more letters out to homes (nursing homes) and explained what the program consists of.

Whether or not this particular subsidized busing program will be continued depends like all mall business upon its showing a profit.

Finally, a program designed to promote customer comfort and convenience, which costs the mall nothing, and is very good for publicity and public relations is the "Mall Walkers" program. Like the busing program, it is sponsored but not organized by mall personnel, and is designed (apart from its public service aspect) to draw customers to the mall.

Manager: The Mall Walkers Program we initiated a few years ago has been quite successful. (This program)...we initiated with Community General Hospital...whereby older, retired people come in and walk because they are disabled in some way such as heart patients and your diabetes. They spend a lot of time in the winter walking because it's cold (outside) so they come to the mall to walk, and we hope that they will shop. They tell their friends about it, and their daughters, and nephews and nieces, and they all come in.

This program is likely to survive. After all, it costs the mall nothing, and creates good will, free publicity, and a potential market for the tenants.

Having considered some features and programs of mall life designed to provide for the customer's comfort and convenience, we will move on to a discussion of how malls provide a source of public entertainment.

Entertainment

Entertainment on the Mall takes many forms. Perhaps the most popular among teenagers is the video arcade. Video games as we have seen are not only a source of entertainment but have redefined major merchandising markets, become a public health menace, altered routine family life patterns in the home, and according to some authorities, threatens normal childhood socialization and resulting personality formation.

Video games

Let's begin by considering the range of games available in mall arcades, who plays them, and how they are played. The following is a list of video games at one medium size arcade studied by the author.

Sega Turbo	Space Invaders	Temptest
Polaris	Wizard of War	Space Wars
Pac Man	Moon Patrol	Centipede
Ms. Pac Man	Asteroid Deluxe	Frogger
Battle Zone	Galaga	Star Gate
Dig Dug	Donkey Kong	Tron
Vanguard	Donkey Kong Junior	Frenzy
Robotron		

The above is but a partial listing. New games are constantly being developed and promoted and many larger arcades have more than one of the same model to help reduce waiting time for video game users. In the arcade business, as in the space craft flights frequently depicted in these games, "down time" is money lost.

The reader has probably noticed from the above list that most video games have a science fiction battle theme. The belligerent nature of these games—their kill or be killed quality—have not escaped the notice of medical and social scientists who are concerned with their current and potential negative effects.

> The U.S. Surgeon General, C. Everett Koop said Tuesday that video games may be hazardous to the health of young people, who he said are becoming addicted to the machines "body and soul." [The Surgeon General said]..."more and more people are beginning to understand the adverse mental and physical effects of video games upon pre-teen age and teen age children."

The article goes on to note that, in the Surgeon General's opinion, doctors and psychiatrists are only now beginning to become aware of the "aberrations of childhood behavior" caused by video games, such as "tensions, sleeplessness in kids, and dreams that have to do with the things they have been doing all day."

The Surgeon General, while acknowledging that there is currently no scientific evidence on the effects of video games on children, believes (as do many of his colleagues) that studies now under way will demonstrate these negative effects. (*Syracuse Post Standard,* November 10, 1982)

Apart from studies of childhood socialization, personality formation, fine motor coordination and the physical problems associated with prolonged playing of video games noted earlier in this chapter, there is the question of whether or not video game playing helps one to develop problem solving skills. Here as in most situations there are adherents on both sides of the question. However, little attention has thus far focused on the future political ramifications of prolonged video game play. Even if the

current generation of children are better at solving maze problems as is
sometimes contended, it may well be that if these games have a lasting
effect, they are less capable of solving major political issues. For example, I
would be very wary of having for a president or secretary of state a person
whose childhood and adult video game playing experience the Surgeon
General characterized in this way: "Their body language is tremendous and
everything is Zap the enemy. There's nothing constructive in the (video)
games." Indeed, by far the most popular video game of the 1980's, Pac
Man, accentuates the Hobbesian theme that "the life of man is solitary,
nasty, brutish and short." In terms of the game plan, one is either the victim
or victimizer. One eats or is eaten.

Perhaps a brief description of this game is in order. It will give the reader
who is unfamiliar with video games some rough idea of how they are
played. Basically, the game consists of the player using a "joy stick" (the
double-entendre is not very carefully camouflaged) to maneuver the Pac
Man on a grid of dots. The Pac Man must gobble up all of the dots before it
is "eaten" by one of the four "ghosts" or "monsters" (the good and evil
theme is also offered in bold relief). Inasmuch as you control the Pac Man
and the monsters are controlled by the person who created the game, "The
Pac Man" represents the forces of good, while the monsters (the programmer's creation that is pitted against you) are the forces of evil. There
is, of course, a certain irony in casting the game's creator in this way that
may have escaped the manufacturer's notice. In any case, the Pac Man may
avoid being eaten by gobbling up "energizers" which are located in each of
the four courners of the grid. Upon eating the four monsters, one accumu-
lates points. There are also bonus point opportunities built into the game.
The player starts with three Pac Men and receives a bonus Pac Man after
accumulating 10,000 points. The game ends when all of the Pac Men have
been consumed.

How long one plays depends upon one's skills. Each game costs twenty-
five cents. A quarter may get the novice about two minutes of play, while an
expert may play for half an hour for the same amount of money. Serious
video arcade game players, teenagers who spend a lot of time at the mall
arcades (sometimes referred to as "mall rats") soon learn the programmed
patterns and lose interest in any particular game. When the challenge is
gone, the fun is gone, and manufacturers are constantly obliged to invent
new programs for new games in order not to lose the interest of the serious
would-be-player. Each of these more elegant arcade video games (as
opposed to cheaper and less challenging home versions) costs about thirty-
five hundred dollars. Many "mall rats" live nearby and spend between 15
to 20 hours per week at the video arcade (*Syracuse New Times,* November
24, 1982, p. 6).

By now the reader may have started to wonder where all those quarters come from that the Pac Man consumes like little dots. Teenagers have, of course, many sources of income, but a relatively new and fairly pervasive one is stealing money from their parents' purse or wallet (*Los Angeles Times,* December 23, 1982). This is perhaps more surprising than it should be. After all, if video games are, as the Surgeon General suggests, "addicting," one time honored way to satisfy the economic requirements of an addiction is theft. While the greatest number of video arcade customers are teenagers and pre-teenagers (mostly males), adults (mall personnel and others) play the games as well, normally during lunch breaks.

There is another, smaller group of sometime video game players who "play for nothing." The following account by a colleague's five year old daughter should help solve this mystery;

> J.J: Abbie, did you have a nice day at the mall?
>
> Abbie: Yeh, I played Pac Man.
>
> J.J.: Where did you get all the quarters from?
>
> Abbie: Quarters? What quarters?
>
> J.J: You know, money.
>
> Abbie: You don't need any money to play Pac Man.
>
> J.J.: It's free?
>
> Abbie: Yeh, it's free.

This five year old had no idea that an essential part of the game play, a preliminary operation that allowed for the game to be played in the first place, was dropping a quarter in the machine. Her older siblings had taken care of that and it simply had not come to her attention. As far as she was concerned one "played for nothing." And, of course, in her case, she was right (in more ways than one).

A great deal of money has been made with video games, not only through their manufacture, sale and distribution and the burgeoning "software" home use market, but in the original design of the games themselves. For example, Rob Fulop 24, Robert Smith, and Dennis J. Koble, created six of the first seven games produced by Imagic. All three have since become multimillionaires (*New York Times,* November 22, 1982, p. 1D).

The publication of Video Games books has also proved to be a lucrative business. One article (Walters, 1982) notes:

> The frenzy for these "videogames" has seemingly overnight created an industry that takes in close to $5 billion a year, twice as much as motion pictures, three times as much as major professional sports...Piled atop our desk are more than a score of videogame books, the ventures of nine publishers, ranging in price from $1.95 to $5.95. One book, *How to Master the Video Games* by 17 year old Tom Hirschfield, who

wrote it during a year's break from Harvard, has sold 926,000 copies. Another, *Mastering Pac Man,* has sold 1,500,000 copies.

Video arcades had initially received a good deal of negative publicity. Recently, every effort has been made to counteract this image. Arcades are now better lighted and monitored than they used to be, and many city ordinances now forbid children from playing video games during school hours. While currently doing well, arcades are bound to encounter increasingly stiff competition from the home video game market, as well as "Playcable" (cable television) that will soon offer a service of 20 video games for home consumption (*Syracuse New Times*, November 24, 1982).

Having considered one form of mall entertainment, let's go on to consider another multifaceted aspect of the same topic — promotional schemes.

Promotional Events

While mall managers, tenants, and owners intend promotional events less as a source of entertainment than a means of attracting potential customers, from the mall walker's perspective, promotional events are viewed as "free" sources of entertainment. Promotional efforts take many forms and are often planned and scheduled as much as six months in advance. The following list gives some indication of the range of these events (Callahan, 1972).

Anniversary Sale
Art Shows — Juried, Open, Show and Tell
Archery Demonstrations
Art and Craft Shows
Auto Shows — Antique Cars, Custom Body and rod, Sports Cars
Baby Contests
Back-To-School
Badminton
Bagpipers
Balloons
Baseball
Beauty Pageants
Boat Shows
Book Fair
Boxing Matches
Breakfast Clubs
Bridge Tournament

Career Days
Caroling
Cat Shows
Charity Fairs
Christmas — Decorating, Nativity, Animated Scenes, Santa's arrival, Santa photos, Christmas Caroling
Circus
Clearance Sale
Clowns
Coin Shows
Coloring Books
Columbus Day
Commercial Art Shows
Costumes
Dances — Ballroom Dancing, Square Dancing, Performing

Dancers
Dog Shows
Dollar Days
Easter — Bunny, Diorama, Easter Egg Hunt, Fashion Shows, Easter Parade, Concerts, Easter Seal
Eating Contests
Elephants
End of Month Sale
Fashion Shows
Father's Day
Fiddlers Contest
Fiesta Days
Fireworks Exhibit
Fish Exhibits
Flag Displays
Flower Shows
Flycasting

Football — PPK-Pass, Punt and Kick Contest
Frog Jumping Contests
Fourth of July
Gift Certificates
Give-A-Ways
Golf Demonstrations
Grand Openings — Time Schedule, Budget
Gun Clinics
Gymnastics
Halloween
Hawaiian Days
Home Shows
Horse Shows
Ice Shows
Indian Show and Exhibits
Jigsaw Puzzles
Judo-Karate Demonstrations
Junior Achievement Trade Fair

Law Enforcement Exhibits
Mardi Gras
Military Exhibits
Mobile Home Shows
Moonlight Madness
Mother's Day
Music Presentations — Bagpipers, Battle of the Bands, Concerts, Military Bands, Organ Recitals, "Pop" Festivals, School Bands, Strolling
Openings (other than total center)
Outdoor Living
Pet Parades
Photography Exhibits
Pony Rides
Porpoise Shows
Puppet Shows
Queen of the Mall
Recreation Department

St. Patrick's Day
Safety Programs — Traffic, Fire Safety, Gun Safety, Water Safety, Boat Safety
School Campaigns
Scouts (Pinewood Derby)
Senior Citizens Fair
Sidewalk Sale
Soap Box Derby
Sport Show
Swimming Events
Telethons
Travel and Vacation Show
Treasure Hunt
Trout Fishing
Valentine's Day
Washington's Birthday
Wild Life Exhibits
Window Trim Contests
X-Ray
YMCA-YWCA Events
Zoo (Petting)

These and other promotional schemes help draw customers to the mall and keep them there for prolonged periods of time. While there, many engage in required or "impulse buying." The more persons participating and the greater the increase in sales, the greater the success of the promotional campaign, from the manager and tenants' perspective.

By and large, these special events help to produce a carnival atmosphere (albeit a subdued one) and help to alleviate the normal blase atmosphere that characterizes most mall social life. Some (but by no means all) of the promotional activities suggested in the above list (and some that are not) have been incorporated in Oldtown area malls at one time or another. While tenants typically pick up the bill (through their payments to the mall's Merchants' Association) these promotional schemes usually produce money for the mall, apart from increased sales. In antique shows, art shows, etc., outside merchants must rent mall space to display their wares. While some of these sales potentially reduce sales for mall merchants by creating a temporary source of internal competition for tenants, the increased number of customers drawn by these events, generally increase sales for all concerned.

We have considered in case study fashion how one mall in particular, and malls in general need to provide for customers' safety, comfort, convenience, and entertainment in order to help establish a stable and satisfying social life within the mall. It has been argued that this is a necessary condition of mall survival.

References

Bittner, Egon. 1967, "The Police on Skid Row: A Study of Peace Keeping," *American Sociological Review,* Vol. 32, No. 5, October, pp. 699-715.

"Calgary Crime Wave Blamed on Video Arcade Obsession," 1982, *Los Angeles Times,* December 23, p. 2.

Capaldi, Michael. 1982, "The Ins and Outs of the Summertime Recreation Scene: For Youths the Mall has replaced the old Street Corner." *Los Angeles Times,* Monday, September 6, p. 1, Part IV.

Carpenter, Horace. 1978, *Shopping Center Management.* New York, N.Y.: International Council of Shopping Centers.

Callahan, William W. 1972, *Shopping Center Promotions: A Handbook for Promotional Directors.* New York: International Council of Shopping Centers.

Cicourel, Aaron V. 1968, *The Social Organization of Juvenile Justice.* New York: John Wiley and Sons.

"College Weapons," 1982, *New York Times,* October 31, p. 49.

"Confessions of a Video-Arcade Manager," 1982, *The Syracuse New Times,* November 24, p. 6.

Goffman, Erving. 1959, *The Presentation of a Self in Everyday Life,* Garden City, N.Y.: Doubleday Anchor.

Ksander, Margret, M. 1983, "Delinquent's Norms for Choosing Victims: What Goes Around, Comes Around." Paper read at the Annual Meetings of the New York State Sociological Association, October.

Kuralt, Charles. 1982, a T.V. "C.B.S. Reports" documentary study of The Oak Park Mall in Kansas.

Pollock, Bart. 1982, "Salvation Army's holiday bell ringers getting the heave ho!" *Syracuse Herald American,* Sunday, December 5, p. C2.

Seely, Hart. 1982, "Shoppers unwitting 'stars' of security camera surveillance." *Syracuse Herald Journal,* Tuesday, October 26, p. B3.

"Shopping Centers: Property Rights vs. Free Speech," 1972, *New York Times,* July 9, p. 53.

"Video Games Score Hit at Nursing Home...But they get zapped by Chief Surgeon," 1982, *Syracuse Post Standard,* November 10, p. A9.

Walters, Ray. 1982. "Paperback Talk," *New York Times Book Review,* August 29, p. 19.

Chapter 5

"The Shrinking World"

The Product and Producer of Mall Social Life

In another context, the author has written on the topic of "The Shrinking World" as a way to frame contemporary social problems. There we saw the way in which social problems relate to social theory and are rarely parochial in nature (Jacobs, 1983). There is a certain sense in which one's personal problems are also the product of a shrinking world but on a smaller scale. Allowing that one's personal problems may sometimes stem from wider national and international considerations unknown to the victim, they may be, and are often perceived in a more personal and localized way. For example, old people experience a shrinking (social) world as their old friends die, and the young may have similar experiences when their friends move away, or are lost for other reasons.

Screens, Filters and Everyday Life

Television is an interesting example of this phenomena. While it can be argued that T.V. expands our knowledge of the outside world in some ways, it succeeds in others in shrinking the world of interpersonal interaction. This is true for the young as well as the old. Video games (played in arcades) also have this outcome. Such an activity is essentially a solitary pursuit. Each stands before their own little world, and "plays it." The cathode ray tube however (whether on a T.V. screen, or a video game monitor) does not play back, in the sense that two children play together. In playing a video game, or watching a game played on television, one does not in an interactional sense, participate. "Playing," in an interactional sense, infers the co-presence of at least two participating individuals engaged in a mutually acceptable and satisfying form of play activity. Piaget (1962) and Mead (1934) both understood this. Sitting alone before a T.V. screen or standing before a video game monitor in a darkened room does not meet this minimal requirement.

Since social psychological theory recognizes the need of children to become socialized through traditional interactional forms of play, and how these play forms are essential for childhood socialization and the ultimate production of a competent social actor, what might we expect if these processes become increasingly eroded? What would Mead have theorized about the learning of roles through the game of baseball, if the game of baseball played by the children he observed was "Intelevision's" home video or arcade version? After all, this version does not require the concerted effort of 9 players on a baseball field, but a solitary player standing before a programmed machine. Surely, one is unlikely to expand one's social horizons in this way. Indeed, while the young (and a growing number of adults) experience video games as an enjoyable pastime, the combined time spent by children before T.V. screens and video game monitors and how it results in an insidious way in producing for them "a shrinking world" has, as the Surgeon General noted, thus far received little serious study.

By now, the reader may be thinking: that's a very interesting set of speculations but what does it have to do with shopping malls? Here is the connection we have in mind. We have already noted the general boredom experienced by suburban youth (and adults) and how they seem to have lost the knack of enjoying their own (or others') company at home for any reasonable length of time. Nor are children any longer very resourceful in finding things to do, that is to say, they seem to participate less and less in traditional forms of play with other children that require social interaction and result in social learning and accomodation. We contend that the growing sense of boredom among the young (and adults) may be a consequence of their experiencing a shrinking social world. This in turn, we believe results from the expansion of television and T.V. related pursuits such as video games and the growing home computer market, which adds yet a third screen through which to filter one's social world. This says nothing of the oldest form of screening, "the silver screen" (and the time children and adults spend at the movies) or the "walkman" craze as another way to filter out everyday life. We have seen in chapter 4 the negative physical and psychological effects attributed to the prolonged playing of arcade and home video games. The same is true for many "walkman" users and abusers (Fantel, 1983).

> Like other insidious ailments, hearing loss lies in wait for a long time and sneaks up slowly on its victims. Sometimes it takes years of traumatic exposure to high sound levels before any symptoms become manifest. Yet the vogue for portable sound equipment — such as Walkman-type radios and tape players — has produced an alarming increase of clinically verified hearing damage, especially among rock addicts who like their music loud...

On the street, amid noisy traffic, the listener cranks up the volume to let the music override the surrounding ruckus. He wants the music to blot out the urban melee, to transport him to private islands of serenity. Making the music loud enough to do that, he courts the destruction of his ears....

Unfortunately, the problem of aural damage through loud sound extends far beyond earphone listening. Nobody has yet systematically surveyed the situation in theaters where electrical amplification is used. The nearest index we have is the dismaying fact that 30 percent of all discotheque disk-jockeys suffer hearing damage. Moreover, many otologists believe that the standard set by the Occupational Health and Safety Act are far too lenient and that even below 95 decibels prolonged exposure is harmful.

Nor is the damage confined to the ear. As recent studies have shown, excessive noise increases the general level of bodily stress, contributing to a variety of stress-related physical ailments as well as nervous instability and emotional disorders.

While children now spend large portions of their everyday life in this way, they still do from time to time lapse back into consciousness long enough to recognize their increasing boredom, without being able to focus on its origin. During these intervals of in-the-world awareness they restlessly seek to overcome this malaise. It is in this pursuit that one's local shopping mall seems to hold some potential by providing a social setting for an engaging set of pastimes that one may pursue in the presence of others. While ultimately only another form of the shrinking world, the confines of the mall provide at least some sort of social world, something that T.V. screens, video games, computers and movie theaters cannot do. It is in this sense that the novelty of a different form of social world, the social world of the mall is seen to hold great promise by the bored suburbanite or urban dweller long suffering from the "blase attitude" (Simmel, 1902). Indeed, if large enclosed urban and suburban malls are increasingly replacing more traditional forms of urban downtown shopping areas; and malls even more than urban centers promote (as was previously argued) the blase attitude, how is one likely to overcome creeping boredom at the mall? The answer is, that one is unlikely to succeed at this, but that one is obliged to try for the reasons outlined earlier in chapter one. Worse still, malls are increasingly being viewed, not as one of many alternative settings in which to pursue social interaction, but as the only (or at least preferred) setting for such an undertaking.

You will remember from the first chapter outlining the short history of the growth of shopping malls, that they were intended to filter out the more undesirable elements of urban life. This enclosed cocoon promised to filter out smog, heat, cold, rain, acid rain, or even abrasive social particles such as ethnic or racial groups, persons exhibiting unusual, bizarre or otherwise unruly behavior, and more generally, "criminal" and "undesirable" elements of all sorts. An enclosed social filter of this sort, which promised safety, comfort and entertainment on this scale has not been seen since the court at Versailles. One major difference is that royal courts were private affairs open to a select few, while the goal of shopping malls is to insure inclusiveness not exclusiveness. There is, of course, a subtle filtering process at work on the mall as well, but the social filters are much coarser than those at court and allow for the passage of a greater number and variety of "social atoms." I say subtle because while in principle any respectable law-abiding person can use the mall, it is a privilege and not a right. You will remember from an earlier chapter that malls are private property and that there are different kinds of malls for different classes of people.

The question can be posed: How is one likely to breathe easier in the relatively rarified atmosphere of shopping malls when one found it so difficult to breathe the heavier and more diversified air of urban centers, and this was, at least in part, the "raison d'etre" for the expansion of shopping malls in the first place? There are basically two time-honored social theoretical positions on this question. First is the idea that there exists a "consciousness of kind" (Giddens, 1911). That is to say, people seek to associate with others they feel are like themselves. To paraphrase Disraeli: "Isn't it interesting that all of my friends think like I do?" This school of thought has led some gerontologists to maintain that age and class segregated retirement communities are better social settings for older persons than the more heterogeneous social settings that were formally an integral part of the person's earlier life-style. The former, it is argued, offers older persons the company of others in like circumstances (age and class wise) thus insuring an easier flow of social interaction and less social friction and avoidance (Osgood, 1982, Hockschild, 1973). Others maintain that such settings are a "false paradise" and that most persons residing there are isolated and alienated (Jacobs, 1974). The latter camp would tend to find the innards of the mall too "womb like," and to mix a metaphor or two, the social fetus that finds the comforts of the womb so engaging that it has no desire to enter into the harsher outside social world of everyday reality is fated to be stillborn.

The reader should not overextend the above metaphor and come to believe that the author does not recognize the need of persons apart of the world at large, to take "time out" from the requirements of everyday life now and then. In this sense, going to the mall, watching T.V., or going to Disneyland may provide a necessary and welcome relief. There is nothing inherently bad about any of these (and many other) "time-out" activities. It is not when malls, T.V.s, video games or movies are a part of everyday life that they are a threat to social life. Rather, it is when these essentially solitary pursuits replace everyday life and become "a way of life" in and of themselves that a threat exists. It is argued that, at some point, the quantitative increase in the number of these solitary time-out activities and the time spent pursuing them, can cause a qualitative shift in the "forms of sociation" (Simmel, 1949). Given the above analysis, this change is unlikely to be for the better in that it contributes to the "shrinking social world syndrome," which the individual experiences as some form of boredom or alienation (Seeman, 1959).

Shopping malls, like many other social institutions, have in principle the potential for acting for weal or woe. As a source of convenient shopping, or as a way of providing an occasional respite from the demands of everyday life, they can serve a useful function. However, the individual who pursues T.V., video games, home computer screens or mall walking, in order to escape from the reality of everyday life, is likely to come to no good. Albert Einstein is reputed to have said that he agreed with Shopenhauer, that scientists and artists probably pursue careers in science and art in order to escape from the harsh realities of everyday life. I believe that many persons now pursue mall life for the same reason; but alas, very few have succeeded in this escape attempt (Cohen and Taylor, 1978). It is not easy, perhaps all but impossible to leave for any prolonged period of time the rugged island of everyday life for the loftier world of science, art of mall society. The impingement of everyday life upon the luckless individual is relentless, and I suspect there are as many unhappy scientists, artists and mall walkers, as any other class of humanity.

"Killing Time": Fighting Boredom with Distractions

There is a wide range of activities that persons engage in on the mall in an effort to "kill time" and fight boredom. Some of these will be categorized below in terms of age groups. We will begin with the very young and end with the elderly.

Young Children

Young children frequently prove the exception to that most binding of all mall norms — maintaining decorum. They run when they should walk, talk loudly, holler or cry when they should be speaking in well modulated dulcet tones, hide and/or get lost when they should be close at hand, have temper tantrums and embarrass their parents or grandparents, drop food on the floor or themselves and ignore it, and in a word frequently act somewhere between a social incompetent and a runaway id.

Not all children, of course, behave in this way. Especially on middle and upper class malls some stroll about like "Pinky" or "Blue Boy" or "Little Lord Fauntleroy". But the fact is that children are very different from adults in what they may or may not do, and malls are not designed with children in mind. Four year olds are not big spenders and mall managers, builders and tenants know that. However, the almost total neglect of offerings of some structured and contained diversions for small children on most malls is probably as serious an oversight as the omission of public restrooms. Here again, the newer malls have made some effort to remedy this problem, by including day care centers.

Even merchants who cater to children, like McDonalds, who make provision for the entertainment of children in many of their off-the-mall facilities, have no such proviso in their mall operations. While every effort is made to make the mall a safe, convenient, and entertaining place for teenagers and adults, little if anything has been done to secure the return of small children. From a strictly practical point of view, it may be argued that nothing needs to be done since small children go where they are brought and therefore little provision needs to be made for their enticement. But even if this is so, unhappy children do unhappy parents make. Obstreperous children do embarrassed parents make. Impatient children do impatient parents make.

In short, if being a young child puts one at a distinct disadvantage in mall social life, that is to say, most stores and their contents are for teenagers and adults; and even those that cater to children are frustrating in that children may not touch or buy anything (since they have little or no money); and they must pester their elders to buy things for them, for which trouble they are usually chastised; and their ignoring the finer points of mall etiquette sometimes get them into trouble; and unless they came with a friend, mall life is so structured (unlike a playground for example) that they are unlikely to find one there—there are certain benefits to being a child, i.e., a social incompetent presumed not yet old enough to know right from wrong. This one fact alone effectively frees children from nearly every mall constraint that adults are subject to. For example, if adults were to behave as children, they would forthwith be issued a summons for disturbing the peace (or worse) asked to leave the mall, pay a find and/or appear in court. Add to this relative degree of freedom the fact that children love hamburgers, ice cream, pizza and other things readily available on the mall, (and that they are likely at some point to get them); and that there is, if one utilizes the entire mall, distracting forms of childhood entertainment (even if it is only a child's eye view of the mall from a chauffeur driven stroller) and the reader can see why even disadvantaged and disenfranchised small children often enjoy participating in mall social life, especially when accompanied by friends and/or siblings.

Teenagers

Suburban malls provide a wide range of activities for teenagers. In general, there is very little variation in use patterns within cliques, but some variation between them. Teenagers usually do what their friends do. Nearly all conform to the pattern of rarely going to the malls on weekdays and almost always organizing a jaunt there on weekends. Their infrequent use of the mall on weekdays is due to several considerations, among which are the need of attending school; the press of school work after school; the requirement of being home early for dinner; the scheduled social, educational, and/or artistic endeavors of suburban youth; and the fact that many parents work on weekdays and parental chauffering services are limited to weekends and/or weekday evenings.

While teenagers sometimes go to the mall by themselves (especially those close enough to walk there) they most often go with friends. Most friendships are made at school and with children of their own age group, usually from the same class, and who live nearby. The preferred method of conveyance is to "bum" rides usually cajoled out of one or another resigned parent. This saves each teenager one dollar in round trip bus fares — a dollar more that each has to spend on the mall. Indeed it is a routine part of suburban living that parents spend many hours per week chauffeuring their (and other people's) children to the mall, dance lessons, music lessons, gymnastics, evening school social or sports activities, to the homes of friends, religious instruction, and numerous other "emergencies" that arise in the course of any average suburban teenager's life.

What do suburban youth do when they arrive at the mall? That depends upon a numer of considerations, e.g., are they alone or with friends, how much money they have, which clique they are a member of, the age group they are associated with, what's available on the particular mall they frequent, whether they are there with a specific agenda in mind, or just "killing time," how long a time they have at their disposal, the requirements of catching a ride there or back, whether or not they are asked to chaperon younger sibs, and if it's a weekday or weekend.

Activities

I will begin with a sampling of these mall activities taken from the taped transcribed interviews. This material will relate to two of Old Town's suburban malls studied by the author, the Shoptime and Spendville Malls. The teenagers in this study frequented one or the other depending upon which was closest, and how far their parental chauffering service would take them. Shoptime was (for both teenagers and adults) the more popular of the two. Let's consider the activities of one teenager (call her Julie) and her friends in the course of a typical weekend jaunt to the mall. Julie usually rises about 9 a.m., watches T.V. till 11 a.m. and then goes off to the mall.

First and foremost she and her friends spend "a lot of time" at the (video game) arcade. They often stop in at "The Gift Horse," a shop featuring "jewelry, and design shoelaces and calendars and mugs." They might on these walks stop to visit "The Old Erie Coffee House." Ironically, this is not a place to drink coffee although coffee, tea, and their accoutrements are sold there. However, on these jaunts, Julie and her friends usually have a different agenda in mind, and go there to look at..."cute stuffed animals, the little animal farm, animals, mugs and stuff, cards and pins." From there they might move on to "Sweet Temptation" and get some "gum or something." By then, it would be approaching lunch-time and they would go to the "T.J.'s" (a hamburger place not unlike McDonald's) where they would get a large french fries and coke and sit and talk about a variety of topics to be considered later in the chapter. An alternative to "T.J.'s" is the Pizza Parlor for a piece of pizza and a coke (T.J.'s is preferred by some because the Pizza Shop is "too sterile"). From there they might stop at "Gerber's Music Store" to look at records or sheet music for the lyrics to new songs, and then move on to "Barbara Moss," or some other young women's wear store to try on (but rarely to buy) clothes. By now it would be nearing three o'clock in the afternoon when on weekdays (after school) or on vacation, they might go to the basement of "J.C. Penney's" or "Dey Brothers" department stores, get comfortably situated (perhaps with some popcorn purchased at "Karmel Korner") and watch the "soaps" on television, probably "General Hospital." A final stop on the mall beat, might be a brief stop at the bookstore, not to look at books, but to peruse the latest posters. In short, a typical weekend day at the mall probably begins at about 11:00 a.m. and ends at 4:00 or 5:00 p.m., when Julie and her friends finally return home for dinner.

Topics of Conversation

If the above is a sketch of the typical round of activities that teenagers engage in during a weekend jaunt to the mall, what are some of the topics of conversation that they pursue while mall walking or taking a sit-down break at "T.J.'s"? A partial list is: clothes, schoolwork and grades, school social events, parties, boyfriends and girlfriends, games or sports and one's proficiency in them, "the soaps," vacation trips, and, if alone, with good friends, a wide range of personal problems. Another general category of conversation might be entitled, "put-downs" and deals primarily with dress codes. How it works and its functional relevance and importance to group life will be dealt with later in the chapter within our discussion of the "society of saints." For now, let's consider some of these conversational standbys and how they are generated through that inexorable law of all social life — "one thing leads to another."

> ya, sometimes like if someone walks in with a really nice pair of shoes or something, we'll (say) like I saw them in this shoestore, and really they don't cost that much. My mother said I was going to get a new pair of shoes anyway, that might be what I wanna get. We talk about things that are around us, you know. And maybe we start talking about somebody's shoes and then maybe we'd find someone who's wearing those shoes we know, and she goes to a different school, and we start talking about that school, and keep building it (the conversation) up.

The "Soaps" are another occasional topic of conversation among teenagers.

> ya, my friends usually watch the ones ("soaps") I like too. Sometimes they watch different ones on different channels, and they'll tell me about theirs, and I'll say, oh, maybe I'll watch that when I get home. Because it seems interesting to watch soap operas and compare yours (with the ones your friends watch). Like the other day, I was watching the one on channel 5, and it's so much different (from the one she usually watches). It's not just the different people you see, it's the way they act. And the picture seems so different, the scenery and everything. It's neat to compare them because they're so different.

An interesting aside on the "soaps" and the teenage (and adult) involvement in them, is the way they are viewed, when they are viewed. The experience is not one of *watching* the soaps so much as *living* the soaps. The way in which T.V. and romantic novels are experienced not as a "time-out" activity, but an integral part of "real life" can be had from the following transcribed segment of one teenage interview.

J.J.: Funny books? What's that?
  J.: Things that are real life and are funny.
J.J.: Things that really happen to kids?
  J.: Mmm, ya, books like [that, that deal with real life]. There's this one book I've read about 8 times...it's called *And This Is Laura* and it's about...a girl who lives in this family where her sister is the star of the bowling team; and her brother is head of the debating team, and composes musicals at the age of 12; and her father is a brilliant scientist; and her mother is an author; and she [Laura] doesn't have anything to do, and then she discovers she has psychic power. And she can see what's going on in the future.

Without going into a detailed development of the plot, the reader can probably see by now that the above is not a "typical family," and that the talents of the family members are rarely found in "real life." Here as in our earlier discussion of "the Shrinking World," we see how the escapee from everyday life frequently ends up by confusing the escape world for the real world. Such prolonged delusions, it has been argued, are unlikely to come to any social good. Others have noticed the way in which, "Public relations, television drama, and life become indistinguishable" (Slater, 1970).

Shopping Habits

While teenagers do more window shopping, trying things on, and just "hanging out," than buying, they do from time to time, go to the mall specifically to shop. On those occasions, it is frequently to buy something they were particularly taken with on a former window shopping spree. Apart from personal shopping, teenagers buy gifts for friends and relatives on birthdays and other special occasions. Some, depending upon their economic resources and inclinations are less "impulse buyers" than others and do a good deal of comparative pricing of clothes, records or gifts before actually making a purchase. The shopping habits of the female teenagers in this study were pretty well confined to those shops outlined earlier, i.e., women's wear stores, record shops, fast food eateries, sweets shops, gift shops, an occasional bookstore, and the video game arcades. The male counterpart spent far less on clothing and far more on video games, records, hi-fi equipment, and, increasingly on cartridges for home video games.

Allowing that in the overview teenagers spend a good deal of money, in one form or another on malls, more often than not they go there to "hang out" or "kill time." One teenager put it this way:

> Usually I go up there (to the mall) with my friends to either hang out —
> for something to do during the day because Saturdays and Sundays
> there is usually nothing to do. It's (the mall) someplace to be, some-
> thing to do, it's a nice place to go if you just want something to pass the
> time away.

In some cases, teenagers have friends who work on the mall, in which case they go there to visit their friends as well as "check out" the latest fashions or records. For those who go to the mall alone, i.e., do not go to the mall with friends, expect to visit with friends who work there, or rendezvous with others, there is the problem of chance meetings. This revolves around the notion of acceptance or intrusion. That is, upon unexpectedly encountering others you know, it is difficult to quickly assess whether or not they want you to join them.

> ...I like to go there (to the mall) by myself to be alone for a while: but
> then, it gets too boring, there's no one to talk to. I have to talk to my-

self all the time. Then people start looking at you, well why's she by herself, you know, like I got no friends. And then maybe I'd see my friends and I don't know if I should join them or not; sometimes I don't, sometimes I do...I wouldn't want to force myself on them just to join their group cause they may not want to see me right now.

In short, even when lonely teenagers encounter their friends on the mall, and the prospect of being able to enjoy the company of others presents itself, the outcome on any one occasion, is problematic. Sometimes one joins one's friends and other times one exchanges pleasantries and continues walking on alone. The outcome ultimately turns upon one's snap judgment of whether or not one is likely to be accepted into the group on that occasion, or is about to become an unwelcome intruder. Should one conclude the latter, one continues on alone in the quest for more meaningful forms of sociation.

Decorum

As for the maintenance of decorum, teenagers fall on a continuum more or less where one would expect to find them, i.e., midway between the essentially unsocialized behavior of small children and the altogether proper behavior of older adults. Apart from an occasional outbreak of silliness or horseplay, teenagers are surprisingly well-behaved. The rare exceptions are more often than not lower class black or white teenagers who occasionally come to the mall (blacks and ethnics are not much in evidence at the suburban malls that were a part of this study). These disruptions usually took the form of talking loud and "cool," playing megawatt portable radios at extreme decible levels, occasionally running down mall corridors, and other forms of minor distractions that were not tolerated very long by mall security once they came to their attention.

Another exception to the generally good behavior of teenagers was those who patronized the arcade at the Shoptime Mall (during the period of its first location). The arcade was originally a large double width store located just inside the main mall entrance and directly in front of a municipal bus stop. Loud rock music from the arcade filled the mall common area. The above had several untoward consequences.

First, the oversized arcade held a large number of teenagers and the darkened innards allowed for a good deal of privacy. Dope dealers and other "undesirables" "hung out" there, not only inside the arcade proper but on the benches just inside the door intended for customers awaiting buses. This resulted in the main entrance of the mall having a distinctly unwholesome appearance. It also worked to reduce business for the major mall restaurant located directly across the corridor from the arcade. As a result of this and pressure brought to bear by the restaurant owners, the arcade was asked to move to a smaller, well-lighted space in the basement "service area" that was essentially out of sight and out of mind. This smaller, better lighted and monitored facility, while busy, accommodated fewer customers at one time. There was also nowhere to loiter now within or without since there were no benches on the lower level that one could legitimately "hang out" on.

One informant who worked at the restaurant gave this account of the arcade's precipitous move:

> I heard from someone who had been talking to the (mall) manager and he (his friend) used to work at Cork Steak House, across from the games place — and I heard that they (Cork) squeezed them (the arcade) out, made them move because there were a lot of people, not so desirable types hang out there, and they also hung out in front of Corks.

This in-mall maneuver, coupled with the passing of a city ordinance prohibiting school-age persons from using the arcade during school hours, once again established decorum on the mall.

A final activity of youth (of both sexes) warrants mention. It's actually a form of "hanging out" with a purpose and is referred to as "cruzen." Cruising the mall, is mall walking with the purpose of picking up members of the opposite sex. While some teenagers spend a lot of time "cruzen," their success rate in this undertaking is fairly limited.

Having considered some of the various aspects of teenage social life on the mall, we will move on to a discussion of adults.

Adults

For the sake of convenience and brevity, we have decided to divide the section on adults into two parts — 1) young adults and the middle aged and 2) older retired persons. We will begin with a consideration of the activities of the former and conclude with the latter.

Young Adults and the Middle-aged

As noted earlier, approximately 70% of all mall customers are female. As might be expected, the mix of mall tenants reflects this statistic. On the Shoptime Mall there were twelve shops catering to "women's apparel," eight catering to "men's apparel" and five to "children's apparel." However, this preliminary count is deceiving in that it does not take account of the numerous other mall tenants catering almost exclusively to women shoppers, e.g., Singer Sewing Machine, Sheba's (shoes), Parklane Hosiery, gift stores and the very large women's and teenage clothing sections of the major department stores.

The preponderance of women shoppers should come as no great surprise. Since teenagers to to school during the day and more men than women work (especially in suburbia), this leaves suburban housewives, pre-school age children, and older persons to comprise the bulk of the mall's weekday population. The question may be posed: "What brings these people to the mall, and what do they do when they get there?"

The answer to the first part of this question has already been addressed elsewhere. For the most part, while different age groups engage in different kinds of activities at the mall (apart from the actual need to shop) there is a common demoninator that motivates all age groups, i.e., an attempt to escape from the boredom, trivia or rigors of everyday life. Like teenagers, adult women are drawn to the mall in the search of something to do, somewhere to go, and someone to see — all in a safe, convenient and entertaining setting.

Young Adult and Middle-aged Women

While many of the stores that adults frequent are different from those that teenagers shop in, many are the same. We have in mind here the teen-age girl and adult women's endless quest for wearing apparel. Since women's fashions change rapidly, and suburban women are so fashion conscious, there is no end to their need to buy something. This bottomless pit syndrome is compounded by the four seasons and the fact that suburban mothers not only shop for themselves, but for their children (who are also fashion conscious) and frequently for their husbands as well. This says nothing of gifts for weddings, birthdays, holidays and other occasions, or the practice of buying an item on Monday and returning or exchanging it on Tuesday as a way to idle away the time.

The preponderance of women shoppers should come as no great surprise. Since teenagers go to school during the day and more men than women work (especially in suburbia), this leaves suburban housewives, pre-school age children, and older persons to comprise the bulk of the mall's weekday office, bank, hair dresser, travel agent and other public and private services also draw customers to the mall on a more or less predictable basis.

Other favored activities include women meeting for lunch at the mall. At the Shoptime Mall, favorite eateries and meeting places for women were "Bergsons" (a combination sandwich shop and ice cream parlor) and "Ralph and Erics" (a cafeteria style sandwich shop). Adults generally avoided the teenage hangouts of "T.J.'s" and the "Pizza Parlor." For them, meeting for lunch was a much more formal occasion. Adult women frequently "dressed up" to go to lunch, and/or for a leisurely stroll after lunch on the mall. One teenager put it this way:

The other day I was in here (T.J.'s) and this lady has this really nice fur

coat on...a really nice pair of earrings, and her hair was all elaborate.
Sometimes people can get overdressed for Shoptime. I mean Shoptime
is a nice place and everything, but some people just wear their nicest
things to Shoptime because they want to show off all their stuff that's
nice, and I can understand that.

The incongruity of a well-to-do woman in a fur coat, nice earrings, and
elegant hair-do, eating at T.J.'s is only slightly more incongruous than such
a woman and her friends "all decked out" and having lunch at Bergson's,
or Ralph and Eric's.

The "street corner society" feature of the mall can be found in the
adult's, as well as the teenager's usual round of activities. If coffee shops
serve as meeting places for suburban adults, (especially young and middle-
aged women) the mall corridors serve as a sort of combination boardwalk
and promenade, where one goes to see and be seen, hopefully in the best
possible light.

Let's stop to consider for a moment exactly what sorts of things women
shop for while on a jaunt to the mall. One good example (apart from
clothing) is cosmetics. Women spend more than 12.5 billion dollars a year
on cosmetics "...nearly as much as the Reagan administration plans to
spend next year on food stamps and nutrition programs" (Harden, 1982).
Upper class department stores account for about one-third of all industry
sales, while drug and mass-merchandising stores account for the remaining
two-thirds. According to the vice-president of People's Drug Stores,
"....Cosmetics have no utilitarian value...Cosmetics is a business of hope,
aura and fashion. That's all we are talking about." (Harden, 1982).

The emphasis on "hope, aura and fashion" is consistent with the other
previously indicated major preoccupation of young and middle aged
women, i.e., keeping up with clothing fashions. Both of these efforts are
consistent with their escape attempts from the routine blandness of
everyday life. The author believes that by "dressing up" and "making up"
(activities that women first become involved with in early childhood as a
"let's pretend" game) women continue to pretend to escape from the
routine trivia of everyday life, by making believe that they look and live like
someone they are not, but would like to be. This, coupled to creeping
"ageism" in America, and a concern by the "baby boom" generation (who
are now entering their thirties) that they are getting wrinkles, has led "skin
treatment creams" to lead cosmetic sales. In 1980 $1.9 billion dollars of
skin treatment was sold, an increase of 27 percent over 1979 (Harden,
1982).

Some indication of how desperate the search is for perpetual youth and
an escape from the physical toll of everyday life is the fact that women will
spend $260 for a "La Prairie facial kit" that contains " collagen" and

"elastin" and is "scientifically formulated" to moisturize the skin. This claim is based upon a process developed in Switzerland of "injecting rejuvenating sheep placenta into the buttocks of wealthy and famous people." Women purchase this product even when "there is no scientific evidence that rubbing placenta on the skin will get rid of wrinkles, nor is it likely there ever will be such evidence, according to the American Medical Association." (Harden, 1982)

In addition to cosmetics and fashionable clothing, there is a third major "non-utilitarian" area of women's sales, i.e., the purchase of jewelry. Much of what follows is taken from a taped, transcribed interview with the owner of a southern chain of jewelry stores that are located primarily within shopping mall settings. The purchase of jewelry primarily by women, or for women, is yet another form of "conspicuous consumption" (Veblen, 1979) intended to convince others through our "presentations of self in everyday life" (Goffman, 1959) that we are someone we are not, but would like others to think we are. In short, through these pretend maneuvers, we try to convince others that we have transcended the constraints of everyday life, and that the life we live is interesting, adventurous and exciting.

As is the case for most mall business, women are the major consumers of jewelry. They are primarily the ones who are buying it or the ones for whom it is being bought. Inasmuch as women are the jeweler's best friend, he must rely not only on his own resources, but on those of other stores that cater to women, to bring them to the mall in the first place. A jewelry store cannot succeed without the proper "tenant mix," i.e., stores successful in providing for the real and/or imagined needs of women customers. As noted earlier, there is no magic formula for establishing a proper "tenant mix." Mall managers call upon the same "play it by ear" common sense recipes that store owners rely upon to succeed in business.

The sorts of merchandise that jewelers try to sell women (or for women) is the same kind that the cosmetic and women's apparel business tries to sell, i.e., expensive, high profit items, that will appeal to a woman's (or man's) vanity. The idea portrayed by the purveyors of conspicuous consumption is that the more you spend the more likely you are to succeed in convincing others that you are the one you would like them to think you are. In short, establishing and sustaining deception costs money and the more you spend the better your "escape chances" are. This tacit understanding between the jeweler and customer works to their mutual benefit. The customer is happy to buy those items of jewelry that have the greatest impact on others, e.g., diamonds, gold, or emeralds, and the jeweler is delighted to oblige, since these items have the highest mark up and provide him with the greatest margin of profit.

Most any successful jewelry store depends on its diamond sales:

You have to figure that you'll have half or more of your dollar business (not the number of customers, but dollar sales) in diamonds.... You want the engagement age girls involved. And then your older women, and your middle-aged women (who wear) diamond earrings and diamond drops, dinner rings, and combination sapphire rubies and diamonds. So you're appealing to the whole strata really in the female area. And when you get to the men, about all you have to sell them is an occasional (gold) chain which is something new in the market, or watches, and maybe ten percent or less of the men wear diamond rings, so you have little appeal there. Your primary focus is on the female in the diamond area (the area of highest profit).... Watches have become either the third of fourth (most profitable) item in the jewelry store. They used to be second. But now gold is second, and then sometimes your semiprecious stones.

We have outlined above some of the things that young adult and middle age women do while at the mall. Let us now consider briefly some of the topics of conversation that they engage in while having lunch "with the girls."

Topics of Conversation

Suburban housewives, like teenagers and members of other age or status groups, discuss those things that impinge most prominently upon their everyday life, e.g., what's for dinner, recipes, clothes, the soap operas, whether or not they ought to buy this or that item, their children and grand-children, their personal problems or those of other family members, a good value they found on sale, the wedding or birthday of friends or relatives, and the gifts required on these and other occasions. For those women who are employed full- or part time, work-related topics may be included. These are rarely stories of the usual, routine, or taken-for-granted aspects of work, but are more often of the "can you top this" variety. That is to say, topics are generally related to some peculiar, unusual or interesting feature of one's work life. With these topics, as well as with those noted above, every effort is made to accentuate the unusual and eliminate the routine aspect of the story. All of this is of course consistent with the major concern of all mall life — transcending trivia.

Young and Middle-Aged Men

Thus far we have considered only the women. While the "bread and butter" of mall economic and social life, women are (in this sense) still only "the better half." Young adult and middle-aged men are also involved to a lesser extent, in mall life. Let us see how and when these involvements take place.

As might be expected, men are not much in evidence on the mall during weekdays. The exceptions are those who work as salespersons at the various mall establishments, mall maintenance and security personnel, men who are unemployed or underemployed, those who are self-employed and "make their own hours," and older retired men who will be considered later in the chapter. Women far outnumber men on weekdays from the time that the mall opens at 10 a.m. until closing time at 9 p.m. However, from about 7 p.m. on (after the dinner hour) the number of men increases. They are usually accompanied by their wives and/or children or their lady friends. Adult men, like teenagers, are for the most part likely to frequent the mall on weekends, holidays and occasionally, on weekday evenings.

If we ask, "what brings young and middle-aged men to the mall?" a wide range of answers present themselves. While men do buy things at the mall, they are not major consumers. If it is generally true that teenaged girls and young and middle aged women love to "shop," married men frequently dislike shopping to the point of having their wives purchase much of their clothing, home furnishings, and other essential household items. When married men are seen on the mall, they are frequently there to accompany their wives and/or look after the children while their wives shop. Other times they are there because they are required to drive their children (and/or their neighbor's children) to the mall for an evening or day outing. On such occasions, "while they are there" they spend some time themselves. This gets them out of the house, away from their children, and sometimes their wives, and generally serves as a much needed break or escape from the din or boredom of everyday life. It also serves as a kind of occasional substitute for "a night out with the boys" without the benefit of "the boys."

Part of what makes suburban men poor shoppers is their relatively casual attitude toward high style. While there are several men's shops, shoe stores, and sections of the major department stores devoted to men's clothing on the Shoptime Mall, there are only two or three "fashionable" men's shops. One of these (the most pretentious) recently went out of business, an unusual occurrence on this particularly successful mall.

Another pastime of adult males (both single and married) that is in no way restricted to the mall, is "girl watching." For those inclined, the mall offers a particularly good site for such an activity (or inactivity). We have already seen how 70% of all mall customers are women. This accounts only for outsiders coming to the mall. Most in-house personnel, i.e., those employed as salespersons in the stores, are also women. This has lead some "girl watchers" to concentrate not on women mall walkers who may be seen only for a fleeting moment, but on women salespersons who are essentially "captive audiences" and obliged to stay in the same spot for long periods of time. Security personnel are aware of men who sit in some convenient spot in the common area outside a store and "stare" at salesladies within the store for long periods of time. The effects of staring and its ability to produce stress in primates and humans has been noted elsewhere (Mazur, 1983). Inasmuch as they are not overly disruptive or disorderly, it is difficult to ask this category of "girl watcher" to move on. One nonverbal strategy used by some older in-house security personnel to get them to cease and desist, is to stand in some conspicuous place and stare at the "girl watcher" staring at the saleslady within the store. This almost always produces sufficient stress in the "girl watcher" that they voluntarily, and without having been given verbal or written notice, move on.

A final, somewhat more active form of girl watching that adult males engage in, has been noted earlier in our discussion of teenage activities, i.e. "Cruzen." Adult males visiting the mall as part of the after 7 p.m. crowd may also be seen "cruzen." To provide for a greater success rate than teenagers managed to realize, "hookers" were sometimes seen cruising as well, usually shortly before closing time.

Depending upon the degree of their social isolation, the mall may seem to some men as much a place of interest or distraction as a haven or retreat from everyday life. For example, I recently had a conversation over dinner with a friend of a friend of mine to whom I had just been introduced. He was a psychiatrist, his wife a social worker. This couple lived in a small rural town and commuted into a larger southern city where they both worked. While happy in their rural home, there was only one thing that the psychiatrist saw as lacking to make things perfect, and that was the opening of a large suburban shopping mall where they lived. That would give them (he and his wife) somewhere to go, something to do, and people to see. As things currently stood, their town and home were very pleasant, but there was not much to do there and both he and his wife were bored. It struck the author peculiar, that two well-educated professional people who were bored would seek to remedy this condition by frequenting a shopping mall. We have noted earlier in another context why this would seem in no way peculiar to the psychiatrist and his wife, and why and how the mall might appear to be (even to a doctor) a reasonable remedy for boredom.

To summarize, adult men, single or married, spend far less time and money on the mall than single or married women. Unlike women and teenagers, men rarely come to the mall with friends or arrange to meet them there. Like women (or teenagers of either sex) men come to the mall less as consumers than as casual strollers (or baby-sitters and chauffeurs) and in seach, in one form or another, of an escape from the routine constraints of everyday life.

Older Persons

If many suburbanites, young and old and of either sex, perceive that they are burdened with time and are looking for something to do in a safe, comfortable environment, older persons are especially vulnerable to this complaint. First and foremost, is the fact that retired older persons have a great deal of time on their hands. They neither work from 9 to 5 or go to school from 8 to 3. Secondly, they typically have meager financial resources to draw upon for their entertainment. Thirdly, they are most vulnerable to crime against persons and a hostile natural environment and seek a safe comfortable place to "kill time" (Jacobs, 1974). In these regards and others, the mall provides an excellent setting for older persons. It is climate controlled, safe and comfortable, and provides in many ways for an escape from the trials and trivia of everyday life. In fact, the mall offers older persons what it offers everyone else, but these elements are even more important to older people for all the reasons outlined above.

All of this applies to older persons in general and says nothing of the special uses of the mall. We saw earlier how the mall is used by heart patients and those with other physical ailments as a safe, comfortable exercise area. Such persons are a part of structured programs organized by hospitals and sponsored by the mall. We have also seen how the mall subsidized free bus service for nursing home patients in an effort to do a "community service" and hopefully gain another pool of potential customers who might otherwise go untapped.

Like teenagers and husbands, "Grandmas" and "Grandpas" sometimes serve as baby-sitters and bring their grandchildren to the mall, and are in turn brought there by their own children. This "kills two birds with one stone." It gives grandparents somewhere to go and something to do, and rids harried parents of one source of stress (their children) for hours on end. Finally, the mall offfers older persons a comfortable, safe place in which to meet others in similar circumstances. This allows for interaction, commiseration and the mutual search for meaning.

Summary

We have seen in this chapter how "the shrinking world" is both the product and producer of mall social life. The mall is depicted as one of many kinds of solitary "escape attempts." Because of the expanding use of solitary escape mechanisms, it is argued that people are beginning to feel themselves increasingly isolated. To counteract this isolation and boredom, more and more people are seeking relief on the mall, relief that the mall is unable in the final analysis to provide.

The author has written extensively on the topic of adolescent suicide and suicide in general resulting from an increasing social isolation from meaningful social relationships (Jacobs, 1971, 1982). I believe that the precipitous rise in suicide rates among adolescents in the past ten years can be attributed in part to the expansion of social isolation, which in turn, results to a large extent from the expanded use of the solitary escape mechanisms outlined earlier in the chapter.

We have dealt with what members of four different age groups (young children, teenagers, young and middle aged adults and the elderly) do while on the mall, and what brought them there in the first place.

We will conclude this chapter with a discussion of "The Shrinking World" and "The Society of Saints." Here we will see how the mall, which is used to escape from the trivia of everyday life, only succeeds in further trivializing everyday life, and must ultimately add to, rather than alleviate this major problem of contemporary social life. Recommendations are made, in principle, for an alternative way to deal with this question, apart from "coping."

The Shrinking World and "The Society of Saints"

Suppose that all the social world had reduced itself to one kind of person and that kind of person was a saint. In this unlikely event, we would live in a "society of saints." Durkheim (1938) postulated just such an "ideal type," (Weber, 1947) and related it to the question of deviant behavior, and the universal need in every society for some level of deviance to serve the function of "boundary maintenance." That is to say, without evil (deviance) the recognition of good (normalcy) would be impossible. Durkheim believed that a certain normal level of deviant behavior was required if society was to function. As a consequence, he felt that society had always sought out a range of deviance in order to be able to define and recognize a range of acceptable behavior. So essential is the role of deviance for the recognition of normalcy and the very existence of society, that Durkheim concludes that even in a society of saints, very trivial or minor infractions of saintly behavior would come to be defined as some form of "deviant behavior."

The author will argue that mall social life approaches a society of saints. After all, there is very little untoward behavior tolerated on the mall. As noted earlier, if there is anything unusual about mall life, it is the extent to which "nothing unusual is happening." In a society of saints, nothing unusual would be happening either, in that things would be totally predictable, i.e., everyone would always be doing what everyone ought to be doing according to some strict moral code. This is essentially true of mall social life as well. However even here, as with saints, there must be some recognizable level of "deviant behavior," if we are to recognize the usual and acceptable features of mall life.

As noted earlier, children provide for a certain level of disruptive and/or deviant behavior. In this sense, teenagers and adults can infer acceptable adult behavior on the mall with reference to the unacceptable behavior of children. When one becomes an adult, one ceases to think or act as a child. While this helps provide some guidelines, it does not begin to suffice. We need to provide for other forms of age graded deviance. Not only are adults not to act like children, but they ought not to act like certain other adults. In short, we are required to define an acceptable range of differences, not only between but within age groups. This universal social need leads us to a further consideration of what suburban teenagers talk about while eating french fries and drinking cokes at T.J.'s.

> T.A.: We don't just sit and watch people, but if there's someone funny-looking going by we...um...[talk about them in a derogatory way.]
>
> J.J.: Do you run into many weird people on the mall?
>
> T.A.: Ya, but we (she and her teenage friends) probably have different views of it than you do—I mean anybody who doesn't do things like we do, we think those are weird.
>
> J.J.: Well, what kinds of things are weird—give me some examples.
>
> T.A.: ...people who do their hair weird, wear dumb clothes, or wear "high waters" (pants that are too short), or don't wear clothes that are "in," or people just dress funny or look funny. People who don't dress the way we do, ha, ha.

From this we see that to be labelled deviant does not require that one perform some form of deviant act. Deviance may be active or passive. One need not actually do deviant things. It is enough for one to only look deviant. Indeed, teenagers talk far less about peculiar acts, than peculiar dress. This tendency to make deviant mountains out of deviant mole hills, is particularly prevalent on malls. The reason for this has already been inferred. If one is routinely confronted in one's everyday live by a wide variety of persons, dress codes, beliefs and behaviors such as one encounters in large cosmopolitan areas, one learns to tolerate a wide range of different looks, beliefs and behaviors. Indeed, one becomes "blase" about them. However, if one is routinely confronted by a narrow range of acceptable dress, thought, and/or behavioral codes such as one encounters in suburbia (and its extention—suburban shopping malls), even a small deviation from the norm, stands out in sharp relief. In such settings, how one dresses, does one's hair, or speaks becomes an item of curiosity (and a topic of critical conversation) while such things go essentially unnoticed within the more varied and tolerant social life of the metropolis.

The point is not that teenage mall social life is petty, constraining and intolerant. These forms of sociation can, without too strenuous a search, be found elsewhere. Rather, we have argued that while mall life does not generate these conditions and sentiments, it tends to accentuate them. In short, teenagers (and others) come to the mall in order to escape from the trivia of everyday life, and end instead, not in reducing but magnifying trivia. By constraining, monitoring, homogenizing and filtering out the already low-level of acceptable differences found in everyday life ("variety is the spice of life") mall social life succeeds only in making the dish of life even more bland. While it is true that there is little on the mall to offend anyone, there is little there (in an interactional sense) to stimulate one, and to help provide life with greater meaning. Those who seek this light at the end of a mall corridor, are unlikely to find it there.

The reader may be indignantly considering by this time the seeming contradiction in the author's presentation. After all, we have seen that small children and teenagers like going to the mall, think it's a fine place to "kill time" and even a grand social-institutional invention. However, small children, teenagers and adults all think that a variety of escape mechanisms are fine and indulge in them freely. We have in mind here a wide range of diversions, e.g., T.V., video games, the "walkman" craze, alcohol, drugs, transcendental meditation, mental illness, art, science or rubic cubes. These and a list of others one might extend around the block represent a cornucopia of escape routes that many people like and use. However, this is no reason to recommend them per se.

On another plane, it may be argued that if so many people feel so strongly, the need to escape from the constraints, impositions, trivia or boredom of everyday life, and these escpae mechanisms serve to offer some badly needed relief, why not use them? The author has no quarrel with this position. If everyday life is perceived of as something that it is frequently necessary to escape from, the escape routes listed above will do. However, I have chosen another approach to the problem. Reformulating the question, one might ask, "Why does society not spend more energy trying to change everyday life from something that so many feel that they have to try so hard and so often to escape from?" Perhaps too much time is spent discovering ways to "cope" even to the point of entertaining and "doing" suicide (Jacobs, 1982) rather than trying to change the world of everyday life into a more hospitable place. The author agrees that if "coping" is the goal, then malls may serve a useful purpose. However, if one chooses to pursue the quest of trying to make the world of everyday life a more meaningful and hospitable place to live, then malls (and more generally, the overuse of escape attempts) are unlikely to help. Should the reader feel that the negative case has perhaps been overstated, the following newspaper clipping (Ehmann, 1983) may lead one to reconsider:

This week, a father in Brentwood, California took away his 13 year old's T.V. because the boy was constantly faking illness so he could stay home from school and watch soaps. Within a few hours of the set's removal, the kid got his dad's revolver from the bedroom drawer, wrote a suicide note and shot himself dead. The note said: "I can't stand a day without television. In my heart, I will take my T.V. with me. I love you.

References

Cohen, Stanley and Taylor, Laurie. 1978. *Escape Attempts: The Theory and Practice of Resistance to Everyday Life.* New York: Penguin Books.

Durkheim, Emile. 1938, *The Rules of Sociological Method.* New York: The Free Press.

Ehmann, James. 1982, "As Bad as it Gets," *The Post Standard,* February 10, 1983, p. 2.

Fantel, Hans. 1983, "Warning Lights Flash for Earphone Users," *New York Times,* July 24, p. H19.

Gidden, Franklin. 1911, *The Principals of Sociology.* New York: Quality Library.

Goffman, Erving. 1959, *The Presentation of Self in Everyday Life.* Garden City, N.Y.: Doubleday and Company, Inc.

Harden, Blaine. 1982, "Harvesting the Vanity of American Women," *The Post Standard,* Monday, June 21, 1982, p. B5.

Hockschild, Arlie. 1973, *The Unexpected Community.* Englewood Cliffs, N.J.: Prentice Hall.

Jacobs, Jerry. 1974 (1983 reprint), *Fun City: An Ethnographic Study of a Retirement Community.* Prospect Heights, IL: Waveland Press, Inc.

Jacobs, Jerry. 1971, *Adolescent Suicide.* New York: John Wiley and Sons.

Mead, George Herbert. 1934, *Mind, Self and Society.* Charles W. Morris, ed. Chicago: University of Chicago Press.

Osgood, Nancy J. and McGuire, Francis, eds. 1982, *Life after Work: Retirement, Leisure, Recreations.* New York: Praeger.

Piaget, Jean. 1962, *Play, Dreams and Imitation in Childhood.* New York: Norton.

Seeman, Melvin. 1959, "On the Meaning of Alienation." *American Sociological Review,* XXIV (December): 783-791.

Simmel, Georg. 1949, "The Sociology of Sociability." *American Journal of Sociology,* 55: 254-261.

Simmel, Georg. 1950, "The Metropolis and Mental Life," first appears *The Sociology of Georg Simmel.* New York: The Free Press.

Slater, Philip. 1970, *The Pursuit of Loneliness: American Culture at the Breaking Point.* Boston: Beacon Press.

Veblen, Thorstein. 1979, *The Theory of the Leisure Class.* New York: Penguin.

Weber, Max. 1947, *The Theory of Social and Economic Organization.* New York: The Free Press.